Letters to Mark

Letters to Mark

On God's Relation to Human Suffering ❧ ❧ ❧

JAMES DAVENPORT BRYDEN

Harper & Brothers   *Publishers*   New York

Special acknowledgment is made to the following, who have granted permission for the reprinting of copyrighted material from the sources listed below:

ASSOCIATION PRESS for the generalization of the causes of suffering as stated by Harry Emerson Fosdick in *The Meaning of Faith*, pp. 153, 154. Copyright, 1917, by The International Committee of the Young Men's Christian Association.

THE MACMILLAN COMPANY for the two lines from *Barter* by Sara Teasdale. Copyright, 1917, 1933, by The Macmillan Company.

CHARLES SCRIBNER'S SONS for "The Light of Faith" from *Poems* by George Santayana. Copyright, 1923, by Charles Scribner's Sons, 1951 by George Santayana.

THE WESTMINSTER PRESS for excerpts from *Today*, October, 1949, in the letter of May 16. Copyright, 1949, by The Westminster Press.

Library of Congress Catalog Card Number: 52-11437

Dedicated to

My Wife

Olive Krise Bryden

Why This Book Was Written

It began with a question: "Why is there such senseless suffering and adversity in a world created by an almighty and loving God?"

The man asking the question had been a casual churchgoer for most of his adult life; now, for the first time, he had more than a casual interest in religion. And he wanted, he said, a "straight answer." (Just what he meant by that is explained by the man himself on pages twenty and twenty-one.)

It was a large order. The man, whom I call Mark in these letters, seemed to have the notion that either there was a simple answer that no one had shared with him, or that there was no answer at all and the clergy had agreed among themselves to adopt various subtle evasions of that fact. He was inclined to the latter possibility. The fact is that there is no simple answer; what looks to the layman like evasion may indeed be just that, but it is more than likely to be an honest but involved

7

effort to get at the problem. This book is an attempt to give an answer which many have found to be intellectually satisfying and practically useful in meeting the adversities of life.

By "many" I mean mainly men and women who have attended the course of instruction for adults which I have given for several years from October to June in the New York Avenue Presbyterian Church in Washington. As class succeeded class in the eight-week cycles of the course, it became evident that the question of God's relation to human suffering and adversity must have careful and systematic attention, else progress toward a clarification of basic Christian beliefs could not be made. Accordingly, we called this problem in from the wings of our discussion (where it had been heckling us) and gave it a major place in the outline of the course and in the play of our thinking. Then, feeling that some record of discussions might prove useful, we made tape recordings of some of the class sessions. These recordings have been largely incorporated into this book.

Mark Fisher, my correspondent in these letters, is a composite person in that he represents the many people who have found that the problem of suffering is the mental gap through which their religious beliefs keep slipping away. And at this point I want to commend these people—and their spokesman—for their tenacity in staying with the discussion of the problem; but it should be said also that they did so out of a special kind of enlightened self-interest, for the problem is not primarily an academic one, but arose in their experience, as it does for everyone who believes, or is inclined to believe, in God. It is hoped that those who here participate in Mark's adventure of exploration may find themselves better prepared for their own day of adversity, because they have come to hold their faith in certainty rather than in wistfulness.

The problem of God's relation to suffering is related to every major Christian doctrine and to the profound philosophical and theological questions which lie beneath them. This book, therefore, has rather close limitations, and the insights here should be considered as the beginning of a journey rather than as journey's end.

I wish to express my gratitude to John W. Klotz and Arch Robertson, and to my son, Jim Bryden, who—for my profit—have been my keen antagonists in discussion. I am indebted to Mrs. Martha G. Thorn for her patient work in transcribing the tape recordings, to Mrs. James E. Davis for typing the manuscript, to my daughter, Mary Ann, for assistance in arranging materials and to John B. Chambers of Harper & Brothers for his many very helpful suggestions.

JAMES D. BRYDEN

Washington, D. C.

9

Letters to Mark

"Why Does God Let People Suffer?"

Mark and I had been fishing companions for several years before the outbreak of World War II. Though not a member of my church, nor of any church, he occasionally attended the morning service. During the hours we spent on the streams and lakes of Pennsylvania, we talked of politics and sports and interminably about the international situation, which was then rapidly darkening under Hitler's shadow. But we never discussed religion; Mark wouldn't talk about it, except in monosyllables which made discussion impossible.

He was then a writer for a daily paper which had a solid footing in the community and a good circulation. He seemed content enough with his job—as he said, he did "all right." He seemed content to take the world as he found it without asking questions about life above the level of common sense, but there was an odd restlessness about him. I mean to say that Mark was not a philosopher—or so I thought. I should have remembered that every man is a philosopher under the skin. For the most part, I thought of him as a comfortable sort of fellow, an expert fisherman and a good companion in a boat on a quiet lake at dawn. His occasional attendance at the morning service puzzled me. I'd look down at him from the pulpit and wonder why he had come.

Then one day I asked him why he bothered to come to church when he could spend the time with a second cup of coffee and the Sunday paper. He glanced up from the bass fly he was fussing with and said, "Being a minister, maybe you feel it's your duty to draw me into the fold. I don't want to be drawn into any fold! And I have an aversion to talking about religion. I'm sick of discussion. It never gets anywhere—one question leads to another and so on, until the talk goes into a complete fog, or everyone is at cross purposes and stating exactly what he said in the first place. Religion can be talked about, but not intelligently discussed."

He paused and gazed for a moment across the lake, then turned and said, "Let's say that I go to church sometimes because I like to hear you talk." He smiled as I shook my head. "That may not be the whole reason," he added, "but it's part of it. I sometimes ask myself why I go—and I don't quite know. So let's leave it at that and get on with the fishing." He gathered up his gear and started toward the boat. I followed.

That was our last fishing trip and the last word I had from him until I received a letter after the war, a long time after. Mark had been in the Pacific—we discovered later that we had just missed each other on Saipan. His letter came to me in a downtown church in Washington, D.C. He asked why God lets people suffer. . . .

Dear Jim:

The report in yesterday's *Chronicle* that you are now in Washington brought back a notion I've had, during the war and since, that you might be willing to take up again the conversation you tried to start years ago. You may remember that, on our last fishing trip, you asked why I sometimes attended church and I put you off with the answer that I didn't quite know. That was correct—I didn't. I still go occasionally, but now I know why. I'd like to tell you and ask you a question.

But first about myself, to bring you up to date. I've left the *Chronicle* and am now, believe it or not, raising flowers. Can you imagine me puttering around a green-house? You may remember that my father kept the greenhouses on Kepler Street until his death in 1937. So I know something about the work and the business and find it quite satisfying in a quiet way. I think I went into it simply because I was weary of people and their troubles and wanted to get back to something neutral and elemental and uncomplicated—like the sheer circumstance of growing things. You can understand this, I imagine, from your own experience.

I recall that you once said I was content to be an observer. I wasn't as content as you thought—and that's the reason I went to church. I had no particular faith or beliefs except a practical faith in things as they are and practical beliefs about what makes them tick. But I asked myself a lot of questions about religion. And especially about suffering. That may seem odd to you, but it seemed to me then—and still does—that my question about suffering raises the most central problem of religion. I went to church with the vague feeling that sometime I'd get a clue to an answer and then other questions could be answered, or rather, that the statements of the Church would make sense.

Now, don't get the notion that in any way I'm desperate; I'm not in an emotional turmoil and turning to religion for security. I'm happily married and healthy; we have a boy and girl who present no unusual problems and are more or less well adjusted, as the psychologists say; I get more time for fishing than I did in the old days; and what I don't know about the growing and marketing of flowers my helper does. So, I'm comfortable and quite content—except that I'm plagued by the notion that at my time of life I should be able to tack down in some reasonable form the religious ideas which for years have been buzzing in my bonnet and curiously enough will not be forgotten. I can neither clarify and organize them, nor get rid of them.

And it seems to me a great many people are in just my

case. To this, you may say "of course," but I naïvely thought that everyone else who thought or cared about religion knew what he believed and was reasonably sure of it. This was because I had isolated myself, I suppose, as I did from you, in regard to religion. But I began to talk to people, and found out that a surprising number are so much concerned about what to believe that they actually are backing their interest with cash—they're buying books! The religious bookstore here does a really surprising business.

Some people I talk to don't seem to have come to any conclusions about the traditional doctrines of the Church—except that they can't be shrugged off. They're mystified and woolly-headed and talk the same questions over and over in endless discussions, but come out about where they went in. One Protestant woman I know has given up and turned to Rome for authoritative answers; but I also know Roman Catholics who are dissatisfied with the answers and are reading Protestant books. I know some who have turned to Christian Science, and others who are flitting from cult to cult, mostly of the "self-realization" variety. Some people, of course, say they believe the doctrines—but their belief seems to be nothing more substantial than a passing mood, for the next day or the next week they're still wondering. There's an adult group, for example, in my church—if I may call it my church—discussing the question, "Why Believe in God?" I thought they had come to some conclusions on that last week, but no, they're still discussing it. They've been in the church for years and their uncertainty on this basic starting point of religion confuses me. Still others accept the statements of the catechism, but are incapable of discussing them; their beliefs seem quite unrelated to life and don't seem to have influenced their view of the world or their treatment of people. Their religion is in a mental compartment by itself, and if it is stirred up and disarranged by a question it becomes a jumble of ideas. If there is anything better in religion than this confusion, I want it; or else I want to get rid of it altogether.

As to my own confusion, it now centers in this one question: Why does God let people suffer? My religious beliefs—tentative as they are—are all jumbled together in my mental basket and this question is a hole in the bottom of it; through this hole my beliefs keep slipping away.

Last Sunday the preacher said that God is related to us by "bonds of love," that God loves everybody—and he said it very well for thirty minutes. But there I sat wondering if he really meant everybody. Bonds of love? How does the love of God operate in the lives of people in desperate trouble, the poor devils I saw last week who were burned raw in an apartment-house blaze, not because they deserved it, but because of a defective fuse? And just how does he love the men who are caught in a war which they have not caused and certainly do not

19

want and who, through no fault of their own, will return home maimed or blind or mentally wrecked? To what end does he love the millions of people who starve in India and China? How did he love the bodies and souls of those in times past who suffered the long agony of disease simply because no one knew enough to perform an abdominal operation? Or consider a single case. Just how does God love the nice old lady who fell here last week coming out of church and broke her hip?

Most of the time, Jim, it seems to me that we're entirely on our own and that the love of God is a comforting fiction. I don't believe consistently that it is a fiction —if I believed that I wouldn't be writing this letter. There's something about the love of God which the preachers have missed, or have not made clear. Perhaps they've allowed it to remain hidden in theology. What is that something?

Just about now you'll be shaking your head and murmuring, "Poor Mark." I don't blame you. As I recall, I once said to you that talk about religion never gets anywhere—and here I am asking for it! The fact is that I've never had any straight answers from anyone about religion, and with one side of my mind I still doubt that there are any straight answers, but at times I hope there may be. That's why I am writing this letter—this is one of those times. And it seems to me that this problem of suffering is the place to begin.

What do I mean by a straight answer? I'm not quite

sure, but I think I mean an answer which doesn't back away through endless qualification from intelligent inspection; one which is honest and doesn't scurry into a fog when someone tries to look at it squarely; one which does not depend on a cultivated mood for its validity; one which does not seem true simply because of the voice and pulpit dynamics of the preacher; an answer which depends for its reasonableness on its relevance to life and our general knowledge of reality rather than on its tie-in with other theological ideas in an involved dialectic which I can't follow.

If none of this makes sense to you, Jim, just say so. At any rate, here's my question: Why does God let people suffer?

Sincerely,
Mark

☙ ☙ ☙

June 11
Dear Mark:

Your letter reached me yesterday and I hasten to say that I'm not shaking my head over it and murmuring, "Poor Mark." I'm a bit surprised, but I'm nodding my head and saying that it's high time you got around to asking this and other questions and attempting to get some religious ideas settled. But bear in mind that the settlement of religious questions is never accomplished alone by words and arguments from some ivory tower or observation post; any answers which attain surety and satisfaction for us do so only as they are lived, for that's how answers come to life and stay alive—by maintaining active relevance to reality. If we continue our discussion, I hope it will become clear to you that this is so.

I can't take time now to visit—much as I'd like to after all these years. So let's get on with the business of your letter.

What do you expect me to do, Mark? Surely you don't think I can write you a neat little letter with a neat little answer. I like what you say about a "straight answer"; but, though I hope it may be clear, such an answer will not be simple and brief—as you will see if you want to pursue your inquiry.

I don't know quite where to begin, for I don't know where you are in your thinking. But I imagine you have reached the place where you have rejected some of the common, pat answers—else you wouldn't still be asking this question. I agree wholly with you that your question raises the central problem of the Christian religion; your metaphor of the basket with the hole in the bottom is really first rate. Now, if you will state the problem as you see it and will tell me what answers you have already rejected, I'll take it from there and make a start toward what I hope you will find to be a straight answer.

Yours,

Jim

Dear Jim:

Thanks for your reply. Knowing you, it's just about what I expected—except that you didn't refer me to any books.

I'll state the problem as I see it. We say we believe in a God who is both almighty and all-loving, whose purposes are all good and for our good, a God who is righteous, just and merciful. This combination of attributes sets our problem, for we have a world around us which seems to contradict our belief. How could the righteous and loving God in whom we believe be at the same time the almighty sovereign of this world where so often the evil flourish and the good are destroyed and where strength alone seems necessary for survival? Or, granting God's might and sovereignty, how may we continue to believe in his love, unless we can see how that love is related somehow to the suffering of mankind? In view of the nature of this world and the reality of mankind's suffering, how can God be both almighty and all-loving? And if his power and love are not simply theological abstractions, they must be related to us. But how?

Let's illustrate the problem. What is God's relation to those events we call "accidents"—which, with a curious begging of the question, are called by the insurance companies "acts of God"? The little old lady I mentioned in my last letter was coming out of the midweek service of the church I still occasionally attend. Poor soul! All aglow with one of the few exciting experiences still left her, she slipped and fell on the icy pavement. The chances are that she will spend the last years of what has been an active and worthy life confined to the dreary inactivity of a sickbed, going down gradually, until her spirit gives up the battle in her broken body and she dies. Where is God's love and power in relation to that accident? Did he cause it? Did he only permit it? Or perhaps he has nothing to do with the accident, but has something to do with her. At any rate, any intelligible answer to the problem of God's relation to suffering must be applicable to this accident, must be an answer and a help to this old lady and to those who love her— and to me, just a layman with an inquiring mind.

Do these questions seem either foolish or blasphemous to you? They're not asked idly, for, you see, the old lady is my mother. I think the Church should have an answer. One of my mother's friends called on her several days ago and said: "Now, Helen—you must submit to the will of God." That, I think, comes close to blasphemy!

The accident sustained by my mother has its counterpart in wide areas of life. Storm and flood, fire, famine and freezing cold take their toll in suffering and death across the world; thousands die daily from "acts of God," or live on in misery, bearing in their bodies and minds and lives wounds which will not heal. How is God related to these "accidents"? If he is the cause of them in whole or in part, what should we mean when we say that he is a God of love? On the other hand, if he has no causal relation to them, if he does not even permit them, it seems to me that a considerable part of our world and its life are beyond the reach of his sovereignty. What, then, should we mean when we speak of God as almighty?

While I'm at it, Jim, I may as well extend the problem still further, so when you reply—if you do care to reply at length—you will have seen the size of this problem for me. All suffering is not, of course, caused by accidents. Some is caused by man's greed and aggressiveness and stupidity, by man's "sin." But a great deal of the world's suffering has been caused by ignorance, plain, innocent ignorance. For example, how was the love and power of God related to the dumb suffering of humanity through the long, painful centuries before men had learned to prevent and heal and ease their common, wretched hurts and diseases? How is God related to the history of suffering? And how is he related to the spiritual dwarfing and disintegration which come as consequences of the unwise choices of children and young people—choices which often enough have their roots in the ignorance and blindness of parents, and in the pressures and drag of society? And what does God have to do with the troubles and adversities which strike at us simply because we cannot live our lives in a vacuum—with the suffering which spreads through society to us because the consequences of what people do and say and think will not stay within their own lives?

I think, Jim, that somewhere there should be answers

to these questions, that is, if the Christian religion is amenable to rational statement. I wish I could get away and run down to Washington, but I can't leave my work for some time. Perhaps I may be able to come down later on at a time when your calendar will allow for a good, long talk. For a fact, this business has reached the place for me where the matter of having any religion, vague as it now is, hangs by a thread. And what am I going to teach my children? There's a poser!

You ask what answers to my question I have already rejected. You are correct in supposing that I have rejected the usual, stock answers: (1) that suffering is sent by God as punishment for sin; (2) that suffering is sent by God to test us; (3) that suffering is sent by God to train us, to improve our character.

Concerning the first, it seems to me that, though some suffering comes as the consequence of sin, there is no connection between sin and my mother's fall, nor between sin and a great deal of the misery visited upon mankind—the suffering, for example, which comes as the result of plain, innocent ignorance. I don't know what to make of the other two answers, except that I rebel against them—they're too pat and simple and they place a terrible moral responsibility on God and throw doubt on his love—and for me, on his reality. How could burning the tender flesh of children in an apartment-house fire test them or train them or provide the opportunity or motive for a higher spiritual life?

All the books I've been referred to try to give comfort instead of answers. I want some answers and I think that if the Church has anything to say on this problem, it should be said. If the Church has nothing to say on this problem, I doubt if it has anything to say about anything —except, perhaps, to give us some practical advice on how to make the best of a bad mess.

This is a much longer letter than I intended to write. But I hope you won't be impatient with me. After all, remember that I'm not trained to deal with these questions.

Sincerely,
Mark

✿ ✿ ✿

NOTE: Mark's letter ended abruptly with his signature. Then, as an afterthought, he had added a postscript asking about my family and hoping I had been able to get in some serious fishing. I sent him a brief note assuring him that I hoped to answer his letter within the next two or three weeks.

As I read Mark's letter I recalled vividly a variety of people who had asked me these same questions: the woman I had found kneeling in the chapel for a final, quiet prayer before setting out deliberately to take her life so that her crippled husband might collect her insurance; the bewildered father who

27

had been left by the death of his wife with a broken heart and the task of raising five young children; the teen-agers of my communicants' class, who wanted to know if God had sent another world war to punish us for our sins; the adults in my class of instruction for church membership, who had asked Mark's questions out of their own acquaintance with adversity and suffering and death. In the years of my ministry, these had been the questions most frequently asked.

Finally, I studied Mark's letter and wrote as follows:

§ *§* *§*

July 5

Dear Mark:

I wish I could refer you to some brief, systematic treatment of the problem of suffering. But I know of none. You will find chapters on it in many books, but I know of no single book which is devoted to it and which meets your questions head-on as you have asked them. I don't want to refer you to the philosophers who, within their broad field, treat the problem of evil. So, I'll do my best—though I warn you that we may have a lengthy correspondence! And please remind yourself that you did ask for it.

Let me say that it is impossible to settle this problem

with a pat answer—in fact, it is impossible to settle it once and for all, if by settling it we mean giving it such a final answer that it will not arise again. This problem keeps arising in experience in all sorts of situations and each time it presents some new, jagged corner which threatens to tear the answer previously given. Life is bigger than our little daily section of it and poses problems bigger than the answers we propose; and life never ceases to test our answers.

However, I think we may come to a general position which will be intellectually satisfying and practically useful. But beyond the answer or answers we may find there will still lie the mystery of God; like Job, we may go forward and backward in our effort to understand, but we cannot know him entirely. We shall still need faith which looks beyond knowledge and reason; this faith will not be a blind hope, but a simple and natural trust which, in itself, is not unreasonable.

The heart of the Christian religion, Mark, is not an intellectual formula for the universe, but a strong trust that no matter what comes—comfort, adversity or suffering, life or death—we are still eternally safe with God. You must have read that great passage in Paul's letter to the Christians at Rome: "For I am persuaded, that neither death, nor life, nor angels, nor principalities, nor powers, nor things present, nor things to come, nor height, nor depth, nor any other creature, shall be able to separate us from the love of God, which is in Christ Jesus our Lord." That declaration is the heart of the Christian experience, Mark. Without it, beliefs in themselves are lifeless. Such persuasion is as much a matter of faith as of reason, and with many folk it is not at all dependent on systematic thinking.

Note that Paul says he is "persuaded." He was an intellectual, a systematic thinker, and yet he was persuaded, not alone by what he believed with his mind, but also by his experience of living by faith. His life was not an ivory tower, but the proving ground of what he believed. I take it that what you need is a systematic, intellectually satisfying answer to your problem. But I am warning you that no answer will be satisfying, unless somewhere along the line you acquire a trust in God which will transmute what you come to believe into a way of life which you, like Paul, live by faith. Only then will any answer have a live relevance to experience. In this connection, I recall an illustration used by Peter Marshall of the difference between belief and trust. You might believe that I have the courage and muscular coordination to push a wheelbarrow successfully across a tightrope stretched two hundred feet above the ground. But you don't trust me unless you are willing to ride in the wheelbarrow. So, you must come to trust your beliefs by hazarding your life upon their truth.

I want to say also that you will need patience, for seeking an answer will be like prospecting for gold—we'll not find it complete and whole in one place, but if we go prospecting for it and dig and treasure up the grains and nuggets we come upon, we shall have in them enough of an answer for our need, enough to live on.

Will you be patient with several more general remarks by way of introduction? I am pleased that you seem to see the problem of suffering not primarily as an academic question. By your statement and illustration of the problem, you have shown that it is not raised primarily by the philosophers and theologians as an exercise for reason; the problem has been put to these gentlemen by life itself. It is raised by circumstances, by the drama of events, for anyone who has any belief whatsoever in God or faith in the reasonableness of the universe. Let anyone believe that there is purpose at the heart of the universe —as over against the notion that blind chance brought all this about—and he is sure to ask what the relation is between this purpose, or Purpose, and man's suffering. And given a belief in God, the question is unavoidable. It will come at us, as it has at you, from the events of life —your mother breaking her hip, the people burned in the apartment-house fire, men, women and children caught in a war not of their asking and not their fault, the long centuries of agony before the coming of scientific medicine and surgery. I'm saying, Mark, that this question is native to life and that the problem it raises is, as such, an elemental problem for the Christian religion.

I certainly do not consider your question "blasphemous," as you suggest I might. You have every right to ask it. Professor Walter Rauschenbusch suggests that we have as much right to ask questions about religion as we have to test our food, which we smell with our noses, chew with our teeth and taste with our tongues before it finally goes down. Questioning is a God-given prerogative of the human mind and spirit.

But you say, Mark, that you are not asking your questions out of any sense of desperation, that you are not turning to religion for security. Do you think it is weak to turn to religion for security? I don't think it is any more weak to turn to religion for security for the mind and spirit than it is to call a physician when you are ill, to seek warmth when you're cold, or to come in out of the rain. It's just plain sensible. Let's not begin our search with any lurking sense of pride or self-sufficiency.

Yours,

Jim

⊘ ⊘ ⊘

July 12

Dear Jim:

You don't want me to keep my pride, do you! Let me explain myself. I've observed that many of the people who come to church are cripples, neurotic, insecure people, who need a crutch. I don't need a crutch! But I want to say that I did begin these letters with the honest feeling that I needed help—and by "help" I mean understanding of something which is beyond me. I still need it. I need some straight answers. But I'm not going to say that I'm desperate.

And I've had the notion for several days, Jim, that this problem is not now as urgent for me as when I first raised it. It occurred to me this morning that the satisfaction of working with flowers is the answer to all my questions. Do you want to continue our search?

Incidentally, the flower business is very good just now!

Best wishes,

Mark

❧ ❧ ❧

July 18

Dear Mark:

Of course I want to continue! Don't let your moods dominate your intelligence!

You are correct—there are cripples, all sorts of cripples, in the Church, just as there are cripples in hospitals and doctors' offices. They are the reason for hospitals and physicians. There are also cripples of various sorts walking the streets, conducting the nation's business, looking for peace and tranquillity, afraid of life's tensions, who need to come to the Church. And there are cripples in the Church who can't be healed because they won't admit they need healing; at all costs they must keep their pride intact.

Shall we continue our quest? It's for you to decide: either this is a real problem and you need help with it, or it's not a real problem and you're going to let it drop.

Yours,

Jim

🌀 🌀 🌀

July 23

Dear Jim:

Yes, it's a real problem and I don't want to let it drop. Pride has no place here between us. And certainly, if my deepest persuasion is correct and there is a good God above us, pride before him is out of place. Except, perhaps, pride that he made us?

But still, you should understand that I have no sense of desperation. I think that is because this problem of suffering is not now at sharp focus in the circumstances of my life. That may happen, of course; it has happened at times in the past and may again. During the war, I recall, I improvised some answers of desperation, but I later discarded them; they couldn't survive comfort, I suppose.

Sincerely,

Mark

Dear Mark:

It is more difficult to answer people for whom this problem has come to sharp focus than it is to answer you. They have neither the emotional stability nor the patience for a series of lengthy conversations. Their need is urgent; they want answers on the spot, or they want comfort. I hope, Mark, that when your day of adversity comes again, you will not need to provide hasty, desperate answers. And I hope that you will have answers which will, as you say, survive comfort.

It is curious how our feeling of urgency concerning the problem of suffering changes with our circumstances. At times the problem seems quite academic and we see no point in raising it. All is going well—as we say, everything is under control; we are safe and the world is a friendly place. At such times, if we have any personal religion at all, God's relation to us and to our world is not a problem. It is a reality. All things and circumstances unite in confirming our faith, telling us that he is here and active in our behalf. Then, order and beauty in his universe proclaim him. In our best, our sensitive moments, as when we see the world's loveliness

> And children's faces looking up
> Holding wonder like a cup

it is not difficult to believe in God and his love. All nature, in its largeness and minuteness, seems to move by the finger of his appointments. We have no doubt, then, that he is real, that his love is active; his presence in his world answers our questions before they are asked. Then, Jesus' words, "Take no anxious thought for the morrow," have persuasive backing: this is God's world.

But it is not easy, Mark, to preserve these high moments. We turn a corner of life and, in an instant, face trouble. Life has been simple, now it is complicated; it has been beautiful, now it is ugly. The laws of nature which have appeared to move in a design controlled for our good, now appear as instruments of destruction. It seemed that our knowledge, wits and skills were sufficient for life; they now seem pitifully inadequate. God is hidden behind a curtain of mystery; sorrow, pain, disappointment, heartache and fear raise again the old question: Where is thy God?

The first thing to realize when the problem of suffering arises is that in asking our questions we are in the company of great souls who have asked them before us. They, sharing with us this common, human trouble, have shared also this problem of God's relation to it. It is naïve to suppose that the sages and prophets—those of the Bible, for example—were of such different stuff and lived on such an exalted plane, that they never asked these questions.

Job asked them, though he was "perfect and upright, and feared God, and eschewed evil." Bereft of his children, reduced to poverty, his spirit dragged down and spurred to rebellion by pain, he sits in sackcloth and ashes and cries out: "The arrows of the Almighty are within me, the poison thereof drinketh up my spirit: the terrors of God do set themselves in array against me. . . . My face is foul with weeping, and on my eyelids is the shadow of death. . . . My breath is corrupt, my days are extinct, the graves are ready for me. . . . My kinsfolk have failed, and my familiar friends have forgotten me. . . . Wherefore do the wicked live, become old, yea, are mighty in power? . . . Their houses are safe from fear, neither is the rod of God upon them. . . . They spend their days in wealth . . . they say to God, Depart from us; for we desire not the knowledge of thy ways. . . . Oh, that I knew where I might find him! that I might even come into his presence! I would order my cause before him, and fill my mouth with arguments." Job would understand your questions.

And the prophet Jeremiah, having carried out the divine commission and delivered God's message to Israel, finds himself reviled as a traitor to his people and facing death. Beaten and confused, he addresses his question to the God who had promised to make him "a defenced city, and an iron pillar, and brazen walls" against his enemies. If piety means that we should ask of God no questions, Jeremiah is far from pious as he cries out to the God whose voice has set him on this course of trouble, suffering and frustration: "Why is my pain perpetual, and my wound past healing? Why art thou to me as a false stream and as waters that fail?" That's strong language, isn't it? Jeremiah would understand your questions.

This is a long introduction, Mark, but I offer no apology for it.

You have made a good start toward an explanation of your question by refusing three of the commonest, pat answers. In general, I agree with you, but since they do contain grains of truth, I think we may save ourselves trouble later on if I deal a bit further with them.

1. One answer is that suffering is sent by God as punishment for sin.

This answer you will find running through much of the Old Testament. (I think we shall later have to consider the question of understanding the Bible, particularly some of the conceptions of God found in the Old Testament.) If you will read the book of Job—and I suggest that you read it in the Moffatt translation—you will find that this is the answer given to Job by his friends. The suffering man rejects it and stoutly maintains his innocence; he denies that his sin is commensurate with his suffering and he will not admit such guilt even to placate God—that would be cowardice. He cries out: "Till I die I will not remove my integrity from me" —I will not pretend to accept an answer which I do not believe!

But, Mark, there is some truth in this answer. It is clear that some trouble and suffering are the direct and indirect consequences of sin; some illnesses, for example, come swiftly or after a lapse of years, as the consequence of misspending our energies or mistreating our bodies; economic losses and dislocations of life sometimes are the results of sin. It is obvious that the wages of sin is sometimes death, that crime does not always pay the criminal as he expects to be paid. We may say, too, that though the consequences of sin are not always in the form of obvious trouble, they are nevertheless real and irrevocable, but for the grace of God—the consequences of lying and stealing, for example, are the alteration and twisting of the mind and personality so that he who lies becomes a liar and he who steals becomes a thief.

So don't get the notion, Mark, that I am anywhere intimating that the God of love is not also the God of judgment. If we accept the theology of the Bible at all, we must also accept the doctrine that the judgment of God is as real as his love. And, it seems to me, such acceptance is reasonable. If there is such a thing as real and decisive human participation in life, if we are not just complex cabbages or glorified puppets, there is also real, human participation in life's consequences—judgment and punishment. And I am not simply saying that the judgment of God is merely a natural consequence, limited and easily overcome—like the pain which follows the breaking of a natural law, or the shattering of a personal relationship by selfishness. No, God's judgment and punishment of sin, but for his redemptive love and mercy, have an eternal extension beyond sin's observable, natural consequences. It must be so, if the soul, the spirit of man, is in any way an eternal creation: the consequences, the judgment, of his life must have an eternal reference. In talking of the love of God, let us not sentimentalize it out of its context in reality; God's love can be real only against the dark possibility of ultimate tragedy.

But when we have made these observations, we are very far from saying that all suffering and trouble are sent by God as punishment for sin. The first difficulty with this notion is simply that it cannot be seen as true —no connection can be seen between sin and much of the trouble and suffering of the world. You are obviously correct in saying that much of it comes from "innocent ignorance." And further, cancer, tuberculosis and the manifold tortures of other diseases are no respecters of persons, but afflict the good as well as the evil and are not generally consequences of sin. This notion is too much out of accord with common sense to be acceptable. In respect to this theory, those events called accidents are aptly named—they strike out of the blue with no relation either to sins of commission or sins of omission.

However, the major difficulty I have with this theory is theological: it does violence to our belief in the revelation of God in Christ. (At this point, Mark, I should tell you that a major element in my position on this matter of suffering is my belief in Jesus Christ as the supreme revelation of God as Love, as our Father.) To say, for example, that God caused your mother to fall and break her hip as punishment for sin of which even she was unaware is to substitute superstition for belief in God's love and forgiveness. I cannot see in such a case how the God and Father of our Lord could let loose upon those he loves miseries which we in human pity would prevent if we could.

It seems to me that the notion that all suffering is sent by God as punishment for sin is not only unreasonable, it is sheer superstition and theologically barbaric. (You may think I have belabored this first answer unnecessarily; if I have done so with you, it is because so many people believe it.)

2. Another common answer is that suffering is sent by God to test us.

First, it must be admitted that suffering and the great and petty trials that flesh is heir to may indeed test us, our endurance and patience, our wisdom and skill in handling trouble, the fortitude of our faith in God and our devotion to what we have believed to be right and good.

But, at the same time, we should admit also that, though suffering may test us, it is quite as likely that the event which causes us to suffer may not test us, but may kill us or maim us or set up a chain of circumstances which places in jeopardy the lives and physical fortunes of those innocent persons dependent on us without really testing either us or them. An accident or an illness, for example, which takes the life of a mother and leaves behind a motherless brood of children certainly gains nothing for the family or community or the children themselves. (And would those who advance this theory claim that such an event discovers for God any further data on human character he has not already known?) Indeed, such an event may even endanger or delay the advancement of the cause of Christ, and in view of Christ's teaching and compassion, we may be sure that it lays fresh burdens on the heart of God.

Let us beware here of a glaring *non sequitur*—though suffering may test in us the spiritual quality which God desires for us, it does not follow that God has sent the suffering or that he desires so to test us. Though I wish for my son a rich measure of spiritual fortitude and though his spiritual quality may be tested by infantile paralysis, it does not follow that I, who am related to him in love, would wish to have him so tested. I would save him from it and if he does contract it, I will bear his suffering on my heart as he bears it in his body. Such is our relation to those we love. Is it not also God's relation to us?

I cannot think that Jesus was using a sentimental, poetic metaphor when he taught us to think of God as our Father. If we earthly fathers love our children as we do, how much more fully must God love his earthly children!

3. The third common answer to the question of God's relation to suffering is that he sends suffering as a means of training our characters and calling forth in us faith in him which otherwise could not be attained.

Here again we must beware of the logical fallacy I pointed out above. It is one thing to say that adversity and suffering are the battleground on which we may win, in accordance with God's purpose for us, spiritually great insights and qualities; it is quite another to say that God, looking upon us, sees when we are becoming comfortably soft and careless, self-satisfied and insensitive, decides that it is time to strike us into wakefulness with disease, to burn down our houses and blast our fortunes. Life itself, with the changes wrought by time, the unstable circumstances set up by the increasingly intricate interdependencies of society and the thousand and one mischances which may befall us—these will provide abundant occasion for learning to meet disaster, these will provide the setting for the creation in us of the spiritual qualities which it is God's purpose for us to have.

I believe, Mark, that God, in his infinite purpose and wisdom as our Creator, has established the general, basic conditions in which his creative enterprise may go forward—not without risk for himself as well as for us; but to say that God deliberately invades our lives with trouble and suffering is to say that he then works contrary to his own purpose, for trouble and suffering frequently crush out the best possibility for spiritual growth. I suppose this is so obvious as to need no illustration. We Christians should remember that the purpose of God's love, as declared in Jesus Christ, is "to heal the brokenhearted, to preach deliverance to the captives, and recovering of sight to the blind, to set at liberty them that are bruised." We may be sure that, in adversity—ours and that of the people of his wide world—God is counting on us for the advancement of that purpose. Let us not attribute to God events and conditions which it is his purpose to prevent or abolish.

For these reasons, Mark, I find unacceptable the most common, pat answers as to why there is so much hellish suffering and heartbreak in a world created by the almighty and all-loving God revealed in Jesus Christ.

In looking back over what I have written, I have the feeling that I have been kicking a dead lion, since you have already rejected these three common answers. But perhaps I have not wasted your time. At any rate, I thought I had better do a more complete job of rejecting them and put us on a common footing at this point.

In reference to the common ground we now share, please do not miss the point that much of my argument against the three stock answers has been from my belief in the revelation of God in Jesus Christ as a God of infinite love. If you do not share my belief, you can hardly profit by my argument. In your reply, therefore, I wish you'd indicate whether or not we have common ground here. If not, I will have to take another line of discussion than the one I have in mind.

Yours,
Jim

❧ ❧ ❧

Dear Jim:

Thanks for your long letter and especially for dealing more fully with the three pat answers. I wanted to reply immediately, but thought I'd better mull your letter over a bit. I've read it several times and have thought about it until it is not on paper but in my own thinking. (The gap between what I read and what is going on in my mind is very apt to be such a large one that I sometimes suspect that the more I read the less I know. This is particularly true when I, a layman, tackle theology.)

Frankly, my reaction to your suggestion that I make a declaration about my belief in God as a God of love is that you are trying to sell me a theology I am not ready to accept. At this point you are using the method which your position as a minister of the Church dictates: you want me to commit myself to a belief of which I am not certain. That's the evangelistic method of the Church against which so many intelligent people have rebelled.

Why not take simply a fair and reasonable approach to this business?

Sincerely,
Mark

۞   ۞   ۞

August 23

Dear Mark:

Very well, let's be fair and reasonable. All I'm asking you to do is to look into your deepest persuasion and tell me if you believe in the revelation of God in Jesus Christ as a God of infinite love. If you don't, I don't see that you have a problem, for note this: what caused the rise of the problem of suffering for you in the first place was your persuasion that the God back of this universe must be a God of love as Jesus Christ declared him to be. I want you to recognize this and to trust your persuasion by giving it the status of a belief. Now, at this stage of your experience, you may not like to use this term "belief." In reply, I suggest to you that a man must come to the place where, with lingering tentativeness, perhaps, he breaks through his uncertainties with a decision to accept his deep surmise. If he wishes, he may accept it as a sort of hypothesis; the important thing is that he shall use it as a serious starting place in his thinking and living. This is the first step in trying honestly to make up his mind and life. In your case, I think this should not

46

be difficult, for you have already entertained belief in a God of love—else you would not have been projected into this inquiry.

All this is fair and reasonable, isn't it?

Yours,
Jim

❧ ❧ ❧

Dear Jim:

I'm quite ready to admit that the problem of God's relation to suffering would not have arisen for me unless I had already entertained some belief in God as a God of love. And yet, as I say this, I am conscious of playing a sort of ring-around-the-rosie: the problem of suffering arose because I believe, but I can't believe—I can't make a solid declaration of my belief—because the belief itself poses a problem which I cannot solve! As I have already said, the problem of suffering is the hole in the bottom of my mental basket through which my belief keeps slipping away. So what do I do?

You suggest that I break through this difficulty by asserting my belief, in faith. I don't like that. Faith would be a strange, new gesture for me; it would embarrass and further confuse me. You should know me well enough to realize that I can't pretend; I've never lived by faith. And yet, declaration of belief in a God of love

—in any sort of God, for that matter—has to be made by faith, doesn't it?

Hastily,
Mark

🄯 🄯 🄯

September 1

Dear Mark:

I'm surprised at you. You say you've never lived by faith. You, a fisherman and a florist! You could be neither, Mark, without faith. And remember the day you signed my note at the bank? You didn't know that I'd pay my debt; you only presumed that I would; you had faith in me. I submit that every time you ride a train or a bus or a plane, you are doing so in faith. Friendships, business dealings, the whole fabric of relationships which gives your life its body, tone and color, are possible only because you have faith, faith in people. Without faith, my friend, you wouldn't have courage to get out of bed in the morning, for the fact is that you could not live the life you do simply on what you actually know. Every day you are hazarding life on what you believe—by faith.

So, relative to the universe itself, that large roof of reality under which you live and move and project your many little faiths—can't you have a belief, in faith, as to the God who created it?

Yours,
Jim

Dear Jim:

I have always thought of faith as an exclusively religious gesture toward God and, possibly, toward life, a gesture made wistfully by folk who like to dream. And here you say that I'm a man of faith. You know, Jim, I believe you're correct. And I'm willing to buy this, now.

While thinking about this, I recalled two words from George Santayana's poem, "O World." The two words "invincible surmise" had stuck in my memory from undergraduate days; here's the poem:

> O world, thou choosest not the better part!
> It is not wisdom to be only wise,
> And on the inward vision close the eyes;
> But it is wisdom to believe the heart.
> Columbus found a world, and had no chart
> Save one that faith deciphered in the skies;
> To trust the soul's invincible surmise
> Was all his science and his only art.
> Our knowledge is a torch of smoky pine
> That lights the pathway but one step ahead
> Across a void of mystery and dread.
> Bid, then, the tender light of faith to shine
> By which alone the mortal heart is led
> Unto the thinking of the thought divine.

Well, I'm trusting my "invincible surmise" and, for whatever it's worth to you, am asserting my belief in God as a God of love.

I've asked myself where I acquired that belief—such

as it is. I am sure it came gradually, for I recall no specific time when it dawned on me, or when I was persuaded that it must be so. I certainly never went forward at a revival meeting. And I've never joined the church. I think this is the elemental belief of a great many people who never state it and have no notion where they got it. It is vague and undeclared and unsupported except by wisps and fragments of other religious beliefs. I suppose this belief in God as a God of love comes from the community as part of our inheritance of the culture of Western civilization.

Sincerely,
Mark

◑ ◑ ◑

September 12

Dear Mark:

In your last letter you said: ". . . I'm trusting my 'invincible surmise' and, for whatever it's worth to you, am asserting my belief in God as a God of love." That's an amazing thing to say!

Your assertion of belief isn't worth anything to me—except, possibly, as a sounder base from which to go on with this inquiry. But it should mean a great deal to you. At any rate, it's your belief and you're stuck with it; I mean that you are going to have to allow it to become the hub of your thinking and live your life around it, or you're going to continue to be the divided, uncertain soul which you now are. And you will belong to a large company; you'll be one more of those who have inherited this great persuasion, as you say, through the culture of Western civilization, and like them you will suffer the division of only half believing it and of never quite giving it a fair chance.

You are divided, you know, Mark. This is shown by the fact that your quotation from Santayana doesn't jibe with the spirit of the rest of your letter. First, you agree with me that you do live by faith; next you say you're willing to "buy" my suggestion that you assert your belief in God as a God of love; then you turn to poetry to express your feeling that your belief is an "invincible surmise," valid because what we actually know is only "a torch of smoky pine that lights the pathway but one step ahead"; finally, you make an outright assertion of belief in God as a God of love—but you immediately stab the assertion to death by saying that you're making it for whatever it's worth to me.

You see, don't you, that you are two people? One of you is a hardheaded skeptic, a scoffer who uses the language of common-sense bargaining to indicate that all this is only make-believe which I may use for whatever it's worth to me in my effort to convert you. The other of you is the man with the invincible surmise, who raises flowers and finds in Santayana's poem the expression of a profound truth regarding life. I suggest that you decide which of these two is to be encouraged. This decision, now, is a commitment you cannot avoid, unless you want to go halting between the two.

Sincerely,

Jim

ᗌ ᗌ ᗌ

NOTE: When I wrote this letter, I knew that Mark would not like it. And I didn't want him to like it; I wanted him to think about it. He didn't write for three months. Then I received a card from Switzerland. He said he would write when he returned home.

ᗌ ᗌ ᗌ

December 14

Dear Jim:

Your last letter jolted me. At first I was puzzled; then as I read it again, I still failed to see what I had done to bring it on. I made three or four false starts at answering it, gave up and started to think about it—and about myself.

"Of course," I said, "I am two people—we all are!" But that didn't help. At night I'd think about your saying that I was a "divided, uncertain soul" and I'd become too angry to sleep. This thing kept teasing at my mind, and

I said, "To hell with it," and convinced myself that I'd been a fool to let "this preacher" get his hooks into me.

My mother died two months ago.

I hadn't had a real vacation since before the war, so Helen encouraged me to follow through on an extravagant notion I'd had for a long time—of going to Switzerland for some skiing. I've blown in the profits of several years, but it was worth it. I'm still two people, Jim; the scoffing skeptic is quite as alive as ever, but I'm not encouraging him. And my assertion of belief still stands —this time, for what it may be worth to me. In saying this I have a feeling that I have burned a bridge behind me.

Before we began our last flurry of disagreement, we had reached the place of rejecting the three pat answers to our problem. But at this point I run aground and am apt to abandon ship. If God is not related to us and to our suffering in terms of those answers, is he really related to us at all? (Right here, your insistence that I assert my belief in the love of God keeps me from sliding away from the problem.)

This is how I see the problem now: as a God of love, God must be related to us, for love is a personal reference to us, *i.e.*, he must love us; but if we reject the three pat answers, we are in danger of seeing no possibility of any relation whatever between God and ourselves and our suffering; we will then have so isolated him from us that we lose him as a personal God and have left only a vague belief in a cosmic deity related to the remote creation of the stars and to the physical engineering of the universe, but not really and directly to us, his children. (I imagine that many people who call themselves agnostics do so because they are stymied at this point—they have given up the pat answers, but have no other answers to put in their place.)

And another difficulty arises here with the rejection of the pat answers. If God is not the one, great cause of suffering, there are many causes, an endless multiplicity of causes. And since we cannot give one inclusive reason for suffering—God—it appears that, relative to human ends and values, we live in a world of helter-skelter forces which have no relation to the preservation of these values, a world which is to us and to all we love a very chaos of risk. And the belief creeps in again that, as far as we are concerned, the world is a chaos; old ladies fall on icy streets, engines fail and airplanes crash, illness invades healthy bodies, fortunes—spiritual and financial—are lost, famine and destitution sweep the earth—all with no regard for evils created or goods destroyed. From birth to death, from the little troubles which bedevil us to the deep hurts which torture us, there is no security or sanctuary for any of us.

I recall how this feeling for the insecurity of human values was expressed by a man I knew in graduate school. A brooding sort of fellow, highly sensitive to the suffering of others and to what he called "the breakage of life's precious things," he gave me the impression of being preoccupied with some deep tragedy. He was. One evening over a cup of coffee, I asked him why he always wore a black tie. He replied, "As a symbol of the essential tragedy of human life." Sounds like Dreiser, doesn't it? And I couldn't kid him about it; he was serious. Incidentally, I've noticed, Jim, that you generally wear gay ties.

Now, to go on. If, after ridding ourselves of the common beliefs as to the causes of suffering, there is nothing further to say, I'd almost be willing to take back again the pat answers. At least, I would then have a world which is not altogether heedless of good and evil, though a world ruled by a God who seems unreasonable in his dealings with us.

Also in this connection, I can readily understand why savages believe in demons as the cause of trouble and suffering—and in a sense I could envy them, for they have at least a personal relation to the powers controlling their fate, instead of having their fortunes confronted by a terrible, mechanical disinterest. Come to think of it, Jim, we still have among us some remnants of superstition, haven't we? The notion that walking under a ladder is in some mysterious way a risk, that having one's path crossed by a black cat is a bad omen—what are these but superstitious beliefs in "bad luck" and, as such means of accounting for trouble which otherwise seem to have no rhyme or reason?

But in a world ruled by a purposeful God, a God of love, a blind, impersonal—and to us, chaotic—whirl of forces cannot rule. Nor can we believe that human values rest upon the whims of easily offended spirits, or on some mysterious "luck." A God of love could not have placed us in such hideous jeopardy!

I want to say in closing that the further we carry this the more I discover that I cannot be as dispassionate and objective as I thought. I feel I really have something at stake. I've definitely reached the place where I find it necessary to put my world together—and I can't do that without using religious ideas. And, as it seems to me now, this is not simply a matter of solving a jigsaw puzzle, which I may work at, or leave alone, as I please. As I say, there is something at stake here: it is a matter of preserving faith—I'm willing to use that word now— that the values of human life—intelligence, skill, love goodness, truth, beauty and all life's precious things— are not just temporary bubbles for which the blind, omnipotent forces of the universe care nothing. I've discovered that I care! And I can't think that they are just bubbles. That's my motive behind all this; the problem of suffering and adversity is the point at which my caring comes to focus.

Sincerely,
Mark

Dear Mark:

My wife joins me in sending our sympathy to you in the loss of your mother. Nothing I may say at this point will help; but I hope that our whole correspondence may place death in a setting which makes it at least more bearable.

I want to return to your remark that, because you have had so little to do with the Church, you don't know how you acquired your belief that God must be a God of love. Let me suggest that, like many others, you have so related God and the Church that you tend to feel his activity is limited to the sanctuary of some church building. You don't state this—you just feel it. Of course, that cannot be so. Though I don't believe that a man can find God as easily on a golf course on Sunday morning as he can in church, I cannot imagine that God must wait for people to come to church before bringing his compulsions upon their souls.

Now, one or two observations on your feeling that once we discard the common answers to our problem, "we are in danger of seeing no possibility of any relation whatever between God and ourselves and our suffering; we will then have so isolated him from us that we lose him as a personal God and have left only a vague belief in a cosmic deity related to the remote creation of the stars and to the physical engineering of the universe, but not really and directly to us, his children."

You've put your finger here on the problem of those

who carry this matter just far enough to rid themselves of the old answers. I recall, from seminary days, the picture of a young student standing in the chapel pulpit, his hands resting on the Bible and his face drawn and shadowed with the effort of thought, praying to "the great, cosmic God," but striving in other phrases of his prayer to hold on to some vestige of his old faith in a personal God. He was using a term for God which took the heart out of his faith, because in his reading he had learned of the danger of making the great God small by anthropomorphizing him. He had depersonalized God and was losing him. Seminary students and thoughtful people like yourself are not alone in facing this problem. Many laymen, once they see and sense the vastness of the universe, come through the unconscious reasoning—or drift—of religious skepticism to the same sort of thin belief in an impersonal deity so identified with the natural forces of the universe as to be beyond caring.

I appreciate the limitations we impose on our conception of God by conceiving of him in any way in our image, or like ourselves; but on the other hand, I am so sure of him in my experience that I refuse to lose him by "thinning out" my conception of him as personal. For myself, an impersonal Deity, with no hearing and no seeing and nothing akin to them, cannot be prayed to and loved, cannot forgive us or call up within us a faith and trust in answer to his loving integrity as our Creator. The universe, from cells to stars, then moves coldly on, careless of human love and fortune, of human need and trouble and suffering, careless of good and evil.

For myself, I would find trust in such a God not only useless, but impossible. In ancient paganism, viewing God as many small gods, there was at least a personal relationship between the worshiper and the god of his choice; and between those pagan deities and an impersonal Deity, a remote First Cause—if that were all the name I could give him—I would choose the former and say with Wordsworth:

> —Great God! I'd rather be
> A Pagan suckled in a creed outworn;
> So might I, standing on this pleasant lea,
> Have glimpses that would make me less forlorn;
> Have sight of Proteus rising from the sea;
> Or hear old Triton blow his wreathèd horn.

I'd rather be a pagan worshiping a little, personal God, than so to lose God among the stars and the forces of nature as to have no God at all!

But I need not so lose him: though I cannot accept the pat answers as to his relationship to life and its adversities and sufferings, I still have faith in Jesus who called God "Father." In daily living, I—and you, Mark—must take a stand on something; if, as fishermen, for example, we're going to make a cast into a stream, we must have solid footing; and I take my stand here on this—that God is personal and our Father. Or, to change the meta-

59

phor, we must have a base of operations, a place we're sure of, if we are to go exploring. Now, we are setting out on an expedition from this base: God is our Father.

Yours,

Jim

ⓘ ⓘ ⓘ

December 26

Dear Jim:

I have a friend who is quite puzzled and impatient with me. He's a young physicist working at a government installation near here. I've been telling him about our correspondence.

"It seems to me," Joe said, "that you and this preacher are becoming hopelessly bogged down—you're asking a question that it's impossible to answer. Why do people suffer in a world created by an almighty and all-loving God? I'd chop off the latter part of the question and just ask why people suffer. Then I could get somewhere—I could answer that. Why bring God into it?"

He brushed aside my assertion that if one believes in God, he must bring God into it. He asked: "Why not just accept the scientific description of the causes of suffering and let it go at that? You know why your mother fell. Let us say that there was a slight change of temperature. When she went into the church, the temperature was just above freezing; when she came out, the temperature was just below and a slick of ice had formed on the pavement. This slick of ice so lessened the friction between the soles of her feet and the sidewalk, that, with other factors due to her advanced age, she could not maintain her balance, and the action of gravity pulled her down. That is not a complete scientific description of the event," he said, "but it's complete and accurate enough to show that we do know why she fell. We know in terms of immediate factors. Why not let the matter rest there? Moreover, that sort of answer is a practical one—preventive measures may be taken by the sexton of the church, and other old ladies may be spared!"

What do you say to that, Jim? Why not let the matter rest there? That's a simple and inviting way to get out of the problem. It's neat, of course; but it's neat only because it's beside the point. And I'll say this: if that's all I have to teach my children, I will feel that I've failed them, either by allowing them to think that God is real, or by failing to give them a decent answer to this question.

Sincerely,

Mark

๑ ๑ ๑

January 2

Dear Mark:

So your friend, the physicist, thinks we're becoming hopelessly bogged down. Before setting out on the next leg of our journey, I think we should give him some time,

61

for he is questioning the wisdom of making the journey. Regarding the problem of suffering, he asks, "Why bring God into it? Why not just accept the scientific description of the immediate causes of suffering and let it go at that?"

He asks this question because he sees no reason for not letting it go at that. He is content, from his point of view, with his scientific description of the causes of suffering —though he may not be so tomorrow. I suggest that the suffering and death of those we love, or a new sensitivity to the world's suffering, tend to make us all philosophers and to set theology up in the very serious business of getting behind the scientific answers with which your friend is now satisfied.

I would say to him further that in being satisfied with his limited answers, from a point of view which does not include belief in an almighty and all-loving God, he is quite consistent. But let him not presume to say that there is no other legitimate, that is, intelligent, point of view. There certainly is!

I imagine your friend would say that we religious folk are fooling ourselves—that we are arbitrarily assuming that there is a God—for the comfort we can get out of it. No, Mark, there's more to this historic faith than that! All of us—including your friend—have before us two alternatives, theism and atheism. The question is, which assumption has more reasonable backing, to say nothing of their divergent outcomes in living, with which we should reckon in choosing between them. On the one hand, if someone like your friend chooses to believe that the preponderance of evidence justifies the assumption that behind this universe there is nothing but blind force and chance without purpose, and that that blind force produced self-conscious beings with purposes, a scale of values, and intelligence which in turn understands the blind force—that assumption is his privilege. BUT LET HIM NOT THINK THAT HIS POSITION IS MORE THAN AN ASSUMPTION.

On the other hand, if we are persuaded that blind force could not have produced us by chance, that there is more behind the rich intellectual and spiritual experience of man, that is our privilege. The point is that in this matter we stand at the place where we look at man in his world and the universe and declare ourselves as to what we are persuaded lies behind them—either blind force without intelligence or intelligible purpose, or a God great enough to have created purposefully this universe and us.

There is no other position, really, except that of trying to balance oneself between these two alternatives—as, indeed, some do, calling themselves agnostics, or, as many others do, calling themselves nothing, but living a practical atheism.

For myself, I cannot imagine—and much less, think— that the long history of mankind, man's upward struggle, the seedlike germination of civilizations, the emergence of skills, of literature and music and science, the friendship and love and self-sacrifice of human beings for

chosen ends, the hope of a world community based on
mutuality and justice—in short, all the values for which
we care, are the result of chance rather than purpose, of
blind, careless force rather than creative intention. So,
with you, I believe in God. And so far from feeling that
we must defend ourselves against the charge of enter-
taining a comforting superstition, I say that the shoe is
on the other foot! I cannot conceive of a deeper superstition—useless and comfortless as it is—than the assumption that there is nothing behind what is so
obviously something. As someone has said, I could as
easily believe that a monkey, given a typewriter, by a
chance punching of the keys over an eon of time, could
write a Shakespearean sonnet.

I should like to know more of your friend, the physicist. Is he willing to say that he is an atheist? I wager
that he calls himself an agnostic—that's the easiest way
of sliding away from the point of this matter, by attempting to split the difference between these two positions.

Yours,

Jim

𝄢 𝄢 𝄢

January 10

Dear Jim:

Thanks for your last letter. I'm beginning to feel that
I now have solid ground under my feet.

You win your wager—almost. I showed your letter to Joe, the physicist, and regarding the first part of it, he readily agreed that we have a choice of only two logical positions, theism and atheism. He said that he is not an atheist, but an agnostic theist, because he knows nothing about God. That's drawing it pretty fine, isn't it? He will not label himself an atheist, because he is not willing to take the position that there is nothing but blind, purposeless, mechanical chance back of the universe, but he still takes the attitude that religious folk are fooling themselves for comfort's sake.

Now, having cleared the way of answers we cannot accept and gotten some solid ground under our feet, I suggest that we look more closely at Joe's suggestion— that we give some attention to the immediate causes of suffering, that endless multiplicity of causes I mentioned in a previous letter. I think we must reckon with them. On the one hand, there seems to be evidenced in them a complete indifference to the values of life. On the other, if we ignore them and take a flight into wishful thinking, saying simply, in the face of suffering, that we must have faith that "it is for the best," we must resign all effort to understand our human lot in terms of God's love and our destiny as God's creatures.

This draws the issue to a finer point, I think.

Sincerely,
Mark

Dear Mark:

I quite agree with you—we should follow your suggestion and that of your friend and take a long look at the immediate causes of suffering.

Why do people suffer? This seems to be a simple question. What are the causes of suffering which lie within the range of our observation? There are two very good reasons for looking for these causes: first, if we want an answer to our question, it is reasonable to look first of all for an answer in the immediate context of suffering; second, assuming the sovereignty of God, it is reasonable to hope that we shall see his intention, his purpose, reflected there.

You are certainly wondering at this point how the observable causes of suffering can possibly reflect the purpose of God in creating this sort of world. Let's see. You said in your letter of December 14: "If God is not the one, great cause of suffering, there are many causes, an endless multiplicity of causes . . . and, relative to human ends and values, we live in a world of helter-skelter forces which have no relation to the preservation of these values, a world which is to us and to all we love a very chaos of risk. And the belief creeps in again that, as far as we are concerned, the world is a chaos. . . . " You then say: "If, after ridding ourselves of the common beliefs as to the causes of suffering, there is nothing further to say, I'd almost be willing to take back again the pat answers." In all this, Mark, I think you are entirely correct. But there is something further to say.

We cannot, of course, catalogue all the immediate causes of suffering, nor would that help us. The problem would still stand. We must look for a reasonable generalization of these causes, which bundles them together, sums them up and points their significance. Though the world is a risky place, it is not a chaos. (If you are becoming a bit weary, thinking that we are beating the air, I suggest that you hold on a bit longer in the faith that God has given us a clear clue to this riddle.)

At this point, we are deeply indebted to Harry Emerson Fosdick for a contribution which takes a long step toward a satisfying and practically useful answer. Instead of a vast multiplicity of causes, Dr. Fosdick sees four, of which he says, "These four things contain all the sources of our misery." They are: (1) the law-abiding nature of the universe and the operation of natural law; (2) human ignorance and the progressive nature of human life; (3) the operation of man's freedom to choose; (4) the togetherness and interdependence of human beings. Let us see, now, how these four factors operate and what their significance may be in respect to human ends and values.

1. It appears that the law-abiding nature of the universe, extending from stars to microscopic cells, operates with unfailing integrity as a system of natural law. Of the operation of this first factor, this first cause of human

suffering, Dr. Fosdick exclaims, "Physical law—what tragic issues its stern, unbending course brings with terrific incidence on man!" Impersonal, careless of the suffering it causes us mortals, the law of gravity, for example, once invoked, brings down the evil and the good. It pulls down the gentle, old lady to the icy pavement, the fleeing bandit when he stumbles in his flight, the workman from the scaffold, the suicide from the top of the Empire State Building. In like impersonal fashion, cold freezes, fire consumes, hurricanes destroy, the laws of chemistry and physics operate with impartial mathematical precision and often leave behind a shambles of suffering, heartache and irretrievable loss. The operation of natural law is the first factor, the first immediate cause of suffering.

2. The progressive nature of human life decrees that human beings shall be born into life with no knowledge or wisdom or skill, without even enough physical coordination to see straight. As infants, we cannot even control our physical functions. Though we live, breathe and move, and are potential persons, we have a long, tortuous way to go before we can become what God purposed us to be—or what we will to be. If we live—if we contract no fatal disease, do not fall from our high chairs, or kill ourselves in other ways—we learn; but not without struggle. How many of us recall the slow torture of mathematics! Though some learning may be an exciting exploration, or sheer joy, much of it is a rugged path de-

manding of us constant plodding. Learning incurs suffering—even learning to walk.

My son took his first steps in the security of our living room. He then graduated to the front porch, then to the driveway, then to the uneven and rock-strewn field beyond. I recall watching him make tottering and uncertain progress to the other side of the field. Red curls blowing in the contrary wind, he'd stagger a few steps and go down. Finally, reaching the other side, he turned and started back. At last, with a little spurt of speed, he recrossed the driveway and sat down on the porch steps to rest. His knees were bloody, but he'd won—and the whole world was before him to walk in.

Beyond the schoolrooms and learning situations of childhood, life is a stern teacher and, as bloody knees may be the price of learning to walk upright, we struggle and suffer toward the mastery of skills and the understanding of how best to live.

To be sure, learning is not always painful, but the fact is that we often fail to learn until the goading lash of circumstance is laid across our backs. And the failure to learn is often painful and even tragic. How much trouble and suffering in the world today need not have been if we, who are of mature years, had learned yesterday!

Furthermore, the necessity of learning rests not only on us as individuals, but on mankind. Until mankind learned the skills of medicine and surgery, human beings suffered and died from what we now consider simple ills. You are entirely correct in saying that a great deal of suffering has been caused by "innocent ignorance."

And at this point, Mark, I must digress from the straight line of our topic and say a word about what I consider a very important implication of this fact. If a great deal of suffering in the past has been caused by innocent ignorance, a great deal of the suffering and a very large part of the social confusion across the world in our time is due to the same cause. It is obvious that the old, elemental sins—selfishness, greed, jealousy and malice—are causes, too, but the moralists are not correct in saying that sin is the only factor in the world's confusions. Part of mankind's suffering and confusion is purely circumstantial, caused by the drag of ignorance —and I don't mean simple individual ignorance alone, but social ignorance and bungling. No good end—peace, for instance—can be attained simply by proclaiming it as a good end; and if we expect it to come in that way, we shall continue to be disillusioned and to blame the failure on sin alone. But something else is necessary. As learning to walk upright depends on learned organic co-ordinations involving feet and eyes, nerves and muscles, so it is that mankind will continue to walk in his present staggering, tumbling way and suffer bloody knees, until he learns the organic communal co-ordinations necessary to mutuality and peace. Until that time, there will be war, with its frightful camp followers—starvation, destitution and death. All this does not excuse our sins—

which are factors in the social confusions and sufferings of our time—and it in no way lessens individual responsibility for taking one's place and doing one's part toward a better future. Nor does it mean that we are on an escalator and must go up—we may, indeed, go down. Man's risk is genuine. But it does save us from a short view; it places our hopes and present failures in the long perspective afforded by man's history; and it saves us from fatuous optimism on the one hand and pious pessimism on the other. We see our place in history—in fact, we make history. We and God make history.

So, we recognize ignorance and the progressive nature of human life as the second cause of human suffering.

3. The operation of man's freedom to choose means that we are endowed with the prerogative of selecting what we shall attend to, what we shall do, what roads we shall take, what we shall eat and drink, what we shall work at, whom we shall marry. And in pursuing our choices, we may let ourselves in for a deal of trouble.

I suppose, Mark, that this is obvious. What wretched suffering and adversity inevitably follow our ignorant, heedless, unwise and sinful choices! Our sins do indeed find us out. The Prodigal chooses to leave home for the far country of bazaars and bright lights, to waste his substance in riotous living, and ends in hunger, shame and disillusionment. Prisons, divorce courts, hospital casualty wards are common settings for the end results of human choices. Poverty of mind and life, loss of homes and home life and reputations and businesses, death and the everyday wretchedness of worry are implicit in the choices and series of choices by which people daily make up their lives. Choices which lead to little troubles and large calamities may appear harmless when viewed singly, but together may be far from harmless.

And it is important to note in this connection that the most ruinous choices are not at first obvious as overt acts, but are composed of fragmentary attitudes adopted and cultivated through the years. Egotism, selfishness, pride, self-pity are compounded of many small choices made below the level of thoughtful, deliberate choice; the attitudes cultivated, the spites remembered, the resentments stored away—these, too, are choices, the more dangerous because they are made piecemeal and so easily assume control of our destinies without our notice. So, we make up our lives and determine what we shall be tomorrow.

Thus, no small part of our trouble, suffering and sorrow comes to us because of this third factor, the power to choose.

4. The fourth cause of suffering and adversity is the togetherness and interdependence of human life. The evil which men do not only lives after them, but spreads around them; our mistakes and blunders, our ignorant and sinful choices, our failures, the accidents which befall us, have results not only in our own lives, but through them in the lives of others. For better or for

worse, we are bound together into families, communities, nations and races—and our togetherness is not simply a matter of proximity, but of organic communal relations and interdependence, so that nothing which we do or leave undone, nothing which we say or think, can effectively be circumscribed within the narrow circle of our own lives. Thus, along the lines of a two-way relationship connecting the people of the world there pass the results of foolishness, sin and mischance; disease, pain, heartache and sorrow will not stay at home, but go abroad into the minds, bodies and lives of loved ones, friends and acquaintances; not to be stopped there, they travel on, finding their way by devious routes into the lives and hearts of strangers.

So, the whole round world is knit together and no small amount of the suffering and trouble we endure has its origin beyond the reach of our power to prevent it.

This togetherness and interdependence of human life is the fourth cause of human suffering.

It appears, then, that suffering and adversity have four causes rather than a vast multiplicity and chaos of causes, as you suggested. In the light of this generalization, does the world look less like a chaos of blind forces?

Now, Mark, in taking a square look at the immediate causes of suffering, as your friend suggested, we have taken him into camp, haven't we? But, at the same time, the difference between him and us is clear; he wishes to go no further, because he sees no reason for going behind these causes, whereas we do. We believe in God, in both his sovereignty and love, and we want to see how his purpose is related to us and our suffering. And I think, Mark, that we are well on our way; I think we shall be able to see reflected in these four causes of suffering God's intention and design. Don't you feel that we are now at the fringe of the answer we seek?

Sincerely,
Jim

*9   *9   *9

January 23

Dear Jim:

Thanks for your long letter of January 17. When I first wrote to you last June, I thought you would chat a bit and bring me up to date on your doings—and would then refer me to some books on theology. But we are moving along. I can see that.

Joe was intrigued and quite "taken into camp" by the generalization—the four causes of suffering—but said he was quite surprised that a preacher should be willing to concede that "natural law, once invoked, brings down the evil and the good." He thinks that this concession will prove too much for us and will be our undoing. However, he is less cocky than he was.

Regarding the four causes of suffering, my first thought was that such a sweeping generalization is arbitrary and could not be supported. Then, I tried to break it down, but could think of no cause of suffering which could not be placed under one of Fosdick's four causes. So, I accept the generalization.

However, assigning suffering to these four causes doesn't settle our problem. Certainly, in the light of the generalization, our world seems less a chaos of forces. But why did the almighty and all-loving God create a universe on this design, so including these four factors as to make trouble and suffering a lifelong hazard and cross for his creatures? And, being almighty, why does he not—even at this late date—eliminate them and bring relief from misery to those whom he loves? And another question arises here: Why does God not act without our begging him to intervene? It's his world, isn't it?

As I've been writing, Jim, I've been wondering how you, as a Christian minister, would attempt with this to comfort a person who is in pain, or is suffering the depression of a long illness. What good would it do to recite to him the four causes of suffering?

Best wishes.

Mark

٥ ٥ ٥

January 28

Dear Mark:

It would probably do no good, for a person in pain or in the trap of deep adversity needs more than a cold recital of the causes of his misery. If he has a back ground of religious experience, I could bring to him th reassurance that he is not alone in his suffering. (Pleas do not think of this as simply a ministerial remark!) Suf fering, depression and fear have the power to close th doors of perception and to confine one to that lonelies of all places—the unrelieved, narrow room of onesel filled with one's own misery. Into this room, no matte how narrow and dark, an entrance is still open for On who will share the pain, banish the fears and care fo the soul trapped in the body's weakness. To see this hap pen, Mark, is one of the great rewards of being a min ister of religion.

But if a person has had no time for religion or for th nurture of a personal religious experience, it is almos impossible to bring him the ministries of religion whe he is ill or in deep trouble. On the one hand, he is in n state to be reasoned with and, on the other, prayer an Scripture reading by the minister are simply pious ges tures to him. Note that I say, "almost impossible." Some times it is possible, because illness and adversity ma break up the hard crust of a person's life, abrogate th assumptions on which he has lived and make him recep tive to the planting of new insights and attitudes. God in his divine solicitude, is his minister, then.

Yours,

Jim

Dear Jim:

Thanks for your last note; I hope that in my last hour of adversity I may have the ministry you speak of.

Now for my questions. Last Sunday I attended the morning church service and heard the minister say— or rather, intimate—that we should not ask why God permits suffering, that that is an idle question. It seems to me that too many difficult questions have been considered "idle"! He warned us that this question is not far from rebellion against God's will and that it has the effect of paralyzing our desire to better the world by meeting it as it is; it sends us off, he said, into endless speculation. He is all for using our wits for getting out of our troubles, and for using science and "Christian social planning" for preventing the miseries which are preventable. Of course, he said this much better and more lengthily than I am saying it. And he appealed very forcefully—I would hardly say persuasively—for more compassion toward those in adversity and need, saying that compassion is the mark of the Christian and without it we ought not to claim to be followers of Christ. I guess it should be counted as a good sermon, but I found it thoroughly irritating.

Now, where do we go from here? It seems to me that we are stuck with these four causes of suffering. Surely you don't think the universe has become a dandy place just because we have generalized the causes of man's misery! Perhaps you believe that on occasion God interrupts the course of the universe—that he interrupts the working of natural law, abolishes the necessity of learning, rescinds our freedom and pulls apart the fabric of the relationships which compose society. If he does these things to lessen the suffering of humanity at his chosen times, to ameliorate our condition, we still face the question as to why he did not contrive in the first place a universe which he would not have to twist out of shape in order to save us from the misery caused by it and by us who are part of it. So, we are back again, it seems to me, exactly where we started.

I'm in a bad mood today, Jim. I've turned a sudden corner and encountered a kind of suffering—I have a beastly cold and am so crotchety and impatient that it's good business for me to stay out of the shop in the greenhouse and let Bob wait on the customers.

Yours,

Mark

P.S. Shall I call on our minister and show him your letters?

❻ ❻ ❻

February 11

Dear Mark:

No, don't show your minister my letters; without your side of the correspondence, I doubt if they would hang together—and I might add that I don't want them to hang separately.

In passing, Mark, I note that you are experiencing in small measure the thing we are discussing—suffering, or at least, discomfort from a cold. I am going to remember later that you admitted it was making you "crotchety and impatient."

No, I don't think that the universe has become a "dandy" place just because we have generalized the causes of man's suffering. A thorn by any other name is just as sharp.

You say that the preacher said in his sermon that to ask why God permits suffering is to come dangerously near rebellion against God's will. I would say that it is only incipient rebellion against what he thinks is God's will. But further, I would say that when one asks that question he is refusing to accept God's universe as he sees it—in effect, he is asking that it be different. That is what you have done in asking why the almighty God does not, even at this late date, eliminate the four causes of suffering and relieve those whom he loves of their misery. And you are not asking for superficial changes in circumstance, but for fundamental changes in respect to these four causes.

Let's have a look at that vague wish to have a world closer to our heart's desire. When one expresses this wish, Mark, he should try also to clarify his wish, shouldn't he? What is the shape of this thing he proposes that God might have made, or might now make? What changes would we suggest, not superficial changes in circumstances here and there, but what we may call structural changes in the universe in respect to the four basic causes of adversity and suffering? There are four possible changes.

1. Because the uniform, impersonal operation of natural law brings suffering to man, would we eliminate it?

Of course we would not! We know that such change, from the standpoint of earthly, human values and of life itself, would bring us complete annihilation. There could not only be no further suffering, there could be no further human experience of truth, beauty and goodness, no life, for the calculable uniformity and faithfulness of natural law are the "operating base" of existence —certainly of life. From the beating of the human heart to the behavior of the stars, this universe is possible only because of the uniform operation of natural law.

This seems so obvious, does it not, as to need no exposition? But, to be sure of our point, let's illustrate it. Let us say that, to spare your mother a broken hip and all the misery it brings, we ask only that the law of gravity be repealed. (Note that I do not say suspended in her case, for our desire goes down to the uniform structure of the universe and not simply to a limited, superficial event.) Just see what follows: We have abolished weight; weights and measures have lost their meaning, nothing will stay in place—persons and things may abruptly take off from the earth and may as abruptly crash back again; no rain will fall; the planets leave their courses to take a chaotic holiday; the whirling earth— if it would still whirl—disintegrates by centrifugal force, and where there were once human life, civilizations and cultures, nations of cities, towns and fertile fields, there is now a mist of drifting dust. Life is over— not only its pain, but all its dreams and endeavor, its love and joy, its character and struggle, its truth, beauty and goodness, with no one left even to mourn their passing.

While we're at it, let's have another illustration. Suppose you are a chemist employed by a paint manufacturing company and have just finished concocting a new type of weather-resistant paint. You leave in your laboratory on Friday afternoon a sample of the mixture ready to be put into production for the market on Monday. But suppose that sometime between Friday and Monday something has happened to the laws of your chemical world. When you return to your laboratory on Monday morning—granting that you still exist and are able to return—you may find that the sample of paint you have made is not paint at all, but salad dressing, or chocolate pudding!

This is absurd, isn't it? And why do you say that it's absurd? Because you can't imagine living in a universe which plays fast-and-loose with you, a universe with no integrity. This absurdity illustrates the fact that we count on the very thing in our universe against which we rebel when we get in its way and it causes us to suffer.

No, we don't want a universe which runs just "anyhow." We shall find no solution for our problem of suffering by so changing the universe that we amend ourselves out of existence. There is no sanctuary from suffering in the elimination of the first cause of suffering and adversity. Though the uniform, impersonal operation of natural law does bring suffering, it also makes possible the sort of world in which persons may live and grow. Obviously, we want that to remain. So, you see, Mark, we have now accepted one-fourth of the universe!

2. Again, in order to abolish the stress and struggle of learning and the suffering which is mankind's lot until he does learn, would we really wish to have God so alter the constitution, the structure, of the universe and our own nature that learning becomes unnecessary? What might that mean for us? What might we be if that prayer were answered?

In the first place, it is possible that we might be something less than human—stones, or vegetables, or at most, worms which feed on the vegetables. We should then have no need for learning, nor should we suffer because of failure to learn. It takes no argument to refuse that as a most unattractive alternative to our human lot!

In the second place, if the necessity of learning were abolished, we might possibly be superhuman, complete in understanding, wisdom, skills, with no failure of our senses—for knowledge would, I presume, still depend in some degree on our senses—no failure of insight, or memory of the past, or vision of the future. Limited as we are now, that state may seem at times attractive, but consider what it would entail. There could then be no process of growth, no advance into maturity, no grappling of the mind with real problems, no exhilaration of purposeful living driving toward worthy ends, no challenge to courageous living, no risk, no hope, no mystery, no discovery—in short, there could be for us in life none of those experiences which now commend it to us and no call for the sort of character which is the hallmark of human nature at its best. The ramifications of such loss might be endlessly extended, but we need only to sum them up by saying that to pray for the elimination of the necessity of learning is to pray for the annihilation of human personality. So, Mark, we are led to accept another fourth of our universe!

3. Again, because freedom to choose gets us and all mankind into such dire trouble and may carry us toward such painful and tragic ends, why did not the almighty and all-loving God create us without such freedom? If,

in complete wisdom and power and love, he had pre-determined our lives, had given us all a perfect set of "built-in" choices, what suffering he would have spared us! And what a lovely, complacent life we should live! But certainly not the life of persons.

Constituted to live without the prerogative of choice and without the suffering entailed by it, we should be puppets: with no ability to choose our way, we should have no selected goals toward which to live, experience no marshaling of resources, no self-discipline, no aspiration toward character capable of achievement; we should never choose a friend, give ourselves to a chosen cause, follow a chosen leader; we should make no plans, nor have need to make them, experience no chosen fellowship in endeavor, no chosen comradeship for disaster or success. We should have a flat, undifferentiated, eternal safety—but we never could be persons. Who would be willing so to resign his humanity? Who of us would choose to be a safe puppet? So, Mark, we accept another fourth of our universe!

4. Finally, because the togetherness of human life, its ties and interdependencies, lets us in for trouble and suffering arising beyond ourselves and beyond the reach of our power to prevent, would we wish to have ourselves so broken apart, so severed from one another, that there could be no traffic of trouble from one life to another? Just think what that would mean! Not only would there be no traffic of trouble from person to person,

there would be no traffic of any sort, for this together-ness which allows such free circulation of man's miseries is the same togetherness which affords the affiliations and ties which bless us far beyond the good things of which mere individual life is capable.

To be sure, these ties make you as an individual highly vulnerable in a society of erring human beings. But would you or any of us really have it otherwise if we could? To lead a safe and placid existence, would we resign friendships, surrender the capacity for love and the joy of it? Would we be willing to go solitary on some lonely way—if that could be imagined!—rather than be set in families? Would we wish to have no familiar folk about us, no society of minds to share life with us, no brave spirits to kindle the fires of courage within us? No, we would not resign so much for safety's sake! We who have known love would not surrender it; indeed, we would bear not less, but more of a loved one's trouble and sorrow.

And when we place human life generally within the perspective these observations afford, we know that we could not live solitarily. Born naked and helpless into the world, we could not have survived alone. And how could we survive alone now? The clothes we wear, the food we eat, the houses which shelter us—all are the products of many hands. The songs we sing, the books we read, the plays we see, the churches we attend, the tools we use, the accumulated learning from which we draw our whole amazing store of blessings, from the commonest mechanical gadget to the complex processes and products of laboratory and factory and the service of the world's commerce—for all these we are in deep debt to unnumbered generations of men and women who have lived and made them possible in that close, reciprocal interdependence which we say troubles us. Who, then, would pray for an utterly solitary life? We surely do not wish the universe and our world so changed as to give us that! So, we take a last step and accept the fourth cause of suffering—the togetherness of human life.

Thus, Mark, like Margaret Fuller, but for a better reason, we have accepted the universe, for the four causes of suffering are also the source of our blessings, and together constitute the structural base of life and provide the only conceivable setting in which human life, character and spirit may emerge, and grow.

It is important to note here, Mark, that this acceptance of the universe is not merely academic: on the level of living where our attitudes arise, the universe is indeed ours for rejection or acceptance. If we reject it, we go increasingly toward confusion and frustrated rebellion; if we accept it, we are on our way to further insight as to its meaning, we form an alliance with it and from this alliance there may arise a new life for us. (This is essentially what happens for many people through simple faith in God.)

Now, Mark, where do we stand? We cease to toy

with the question of why God does not abolish suffering and adversity by changing the universe for us whom he loves; we ask, rather, our original question, but with a still finer point on it: since God so constituted our universe, what may we say is his purpose in it so far as we are concerned and, in view of that purpose, what is his relation to us and to our suffering and adversity? You ask, "And how may we know his purpose?" Let me suggest that we may see his purpose reflected in the four causes of our suffering.

Finally, having in mind one of the practical conclusions we shall come to, I suggest, Mark, that though you are wise in staying away from your customers when you are "crotchety and impatient," there is a more excellent way of dealing with the spiritual hazards of the common cold.

Sincerely,
Jim

۩ ۩ ۩

February 19

Dear Jim:

I suppose that your gibe, "there is a more excellent way of dealing with the spiritual hazards of the common cold," is germane to the matter of God's relation to the universe, but I must say that I think it's a very long shot. So I'll put it down to your preacher's instinct to deliver a bit of a sermon. Once a preacher, always a preacher!

All right, I "accept the universe," though in saying

that I do feel a bit silly. Who am I to go around accepting the universe? But I do see what you mean: The universe is my job, my associates, the material I work with, the resistance I encounter, even the traffic I have to buck during rush hours. So I'll no longer toy, as you say, with the question of why God did not set it up differently, or why even at this late date he does not change it. I hope we'll get around to what acceptance means when one is faced with adversity, not simply personal adversity, but a world which seems all wrong, or wrong where I might be trying to set it right. This will be the problem: how does one "accept the universe" and at the same time rebel, as he should, against the conditions in our world which do violence to the values of human personality? Acceptance of the universe may eventuate in acceptance of things as they are—as in India, for example, or in respect to some odorous political practice or an evil social condition here which cries out for correction. May not acceptance cut the nerve of concern? I suppose the difference between acceptance which is content to do nothing and acceptance within which one still retains the capacity for social concern and action lies in what one conceives to be the relation of God to things as they are. And that is just what we're after, isn't it? We want to know God's purpose.

For the first time in our correspondence, I'm becoming, with you, a protagonist for this view you're developing. I think I have something to offer, in regard to our question as you put it at the end of your last letter: "Since God so constituted our universe, what may we say is his purpose in it so far as we are concerned and, in view of that purpose, what is his relation to us and to our suffering and adversity?" In regard to the first part of that question—as to God's purpose—it seems to me that we may answer it something like this: since God created this setting for life, and the four causes of suffering constitute the only conceivable setting in which human life—persons—may emerge and grow, it must be that the purpose of God is the creation of persons. Simple, isn't it? Or is something wrong with my logic?

Someone will say to this: "Of course, God's purpose is the creation of persons; no lengthy argument is necessary to back that statement. That's what the Church has been saying all along." My reply is that there is considerable difference for me between that being said by the Church out of its centuries of faith—and what you may call the "dialectic" of faith in experience—and my assertion of it out of a new conviction that it must be so! The difference is that I, for whom the doctrines of the church have had little relevance to the real problems of life, am now more prepared to trust God in a way which was not possible before. (Knowing me, don't you think this is quite a step? Note that I say that I am more prepared to trust God; I have a sort of mental trust, but am not sure what such trust may mean for me in daily living where one's religion must come to focus and make a difference.

The growth of my faith in God is still inhibited by

two questions. I accept the sufferings of mankind as a sort of tragic necessity, the price of the creation of persons which is the purpose of God, but what is God's relation to this process of creation and to the suffering it entails? That is my first question. I suppose I am asking again the old question of the mocker in the Psalms, "Where is thy God?" That is, what does God really have to do with you and your suffering? You say you have faith in him. I ask, "How does he answer your faith?"

My second question is: What is the practical use of this view wherein I accept adversity and suffering as the price of the creation of persons? What do I do beyond such acceptance? It seems to me that I have now reached a position quite like that of the Stoics. Admitted that the acceptance of suffering without rebellion or whining may allow one to meet life with added dignity, it has always seemed to me that the dignity of the Stoic is a rather hollow pose. Certainly one may create a mood, but I need more than a mood to meet life. What is it I need? I'm not sure, but it seems that I need to feel a companionship with God in his creation, to feel that we are somehow together. This is a very old desire—isn't it—this desire in the heart of man to feel an at-one-ment with his God? But—and this again is the point where I now stick fast—what is God's relation to me and what do I do beyond accepting suffering and adversity?

Sincerely,

Mark

Dear Mark:

Going directly to your first question: the first and basic thing we may be sure of is that God's relation to us and to our adversity and suffering is determined by his nature.

Now, we need not feel that we are presumptuous in speaking of the nature of God. (Don't allow this parenthetical remark to trouble you. I insert it because in your reading you may have dipped into some of the books of certain current theologians who are being widely read and followed. In their fervent rejection of the liberal idea that God is immanent within the universe, they contend that he is so utterly transcendent as to be entirely beyond our ken. I feel that this notion, in its extreme statements, is essentially the position of eighteenth-century deism—you might pause to look up "deism" in your encyclopedia—and that it arises in our time from disillusionment with the liberal promise that ready access to God guarantees a better world. The proponents of this view seem to feel that since there can now be no good promise that a better world is just around the corner, it must be that God is remote, rather than near, utterly transcendent, rather than within the reach of our minds and experience. This conclusion is a *non sequitur;* but it is not harmless, for it is directed not only against the extreme liberal view of God's immanence, but also against the heart of traditional orthodoxy—that God may be known and experienced.)

Certainly we cannot comprehend God entirely; he is too great for us. But we can see the fringe of his garment. Beginning with the world as we find it, and in view of our persuasion, our faith, that God created it, we have every right to reason about his nature. Consider, then, several propositions. Please consider them carefully.

1. The first thing we may say about God is that he is indeed a great God.

When man knew little about the world in which he lived, when it was a small world, fragmented by his ignorance and compressed within the narrow limits of his meager understanding, he saw it and his fortunes as controlled by many little gods; a little world and little gods went easily together. And as the world was divided by man's split-up comprehension of it, so its Creator was divided to man's mind into many gods; it was no accident that primitive religion was polytheistic.

But as our comprehension of the world grew, as it became part of a universe in our view of it, it dawned on us that it could not be accounted for by these many little gods in which we believed. (When I say that it dawned on us, I simply mean that that insight came; and I am not forgetting the great Biblical doctrine that God revealed himself; it could not have dawned on us at all if he had not revealed himself.) The French philosopher Comte once said that with the advancement of science the day would come when man would escort God to the edge of the universe and bow him out with thanks for his provisional services. How incorrect that prophecy was! So far from seeing all deity vanish, we have seen God in our view and comprehension grow great beyond our imagining. We know that, as Creator of a universe such as this, our God must be a great God indeed! Now, with the magnitude of the universe outreaching our imagination and its amazing complexity raising limitless expectation of wonders yet unknown, we say with conviction: "Surely, the Lord is a great God." Greatness is a corollary of his existence.

2. Further, as a great God, he must be a God of great and continuing purpose who has not set out lightly on this enterprise of creation and will not lightly abandon it. He cannot be simply the Starter, or great First Cause, of his universe; we cannot think of him as having begun something here and then abandoned it as a child may abandon some passing interest. We cannot think of shallowness of purpose and the greatness of God as going together.

Even casual observation of the course of human history, and of what has here emerged, points to an unfolding purpose and gives this proposition backing. In a world where man's first music was made by the thumping of a club on a hollow log, then by drums, then by reeds and pipes, then by trumpets and simple strings, then by harpsichords, pianos and organs, and at last by orchestras playing great symphonies—in such a world there seems to be an ascending purpose. At least, it seems so to me. In a world where natural law maintains a constant, calculable integrity and the mind of man has moved from superstition to science, from savagery into a widening comprehension of good ends, effective means and the building of civilizations, though we may not know where it all is going, we do see undeniably that a purpose is here unfolding.

God could not be truly great—as he, the Creator of this universe must be—were he not a God of great and continuing purpose. Purposefulness is a corollary of greatness.

3. Since the four causes of human suffering constitute together the only conceivable setting in which the creation of persons is possible, we may say that God's purpose is the creation of persons and that that is the stake he has in this enterprise. (You stated this, Mark, in your last letter. I have simply stated it again in order to relate it to the foregoing propositions and to the one which follows.)

4. One more step is necessary to come to firm grips with the question of God's relation to us and our adversity and suffering. The answer is implicit in the three preceding propositions: a God great enough to have created this universe, a purposeful God who has crowned his creation by the creation of persons in his own image, must be a God of infinite love, else he were monstrous. It is impossible to think of our God as not caring for his

creation. Love is a corollary of his greatness and is on the scale of the universe itself, limitless, beyond our power to grasp, concerned beyond our power to appreciate. This, of course, is what the New Testament teaches: "GOD IS LOVE."

This, Mark, is our answer to your question as to God's relation to us and to our adversity and suffering. God has with us a relation of infinite love. However, we still have some way to go, and you indicated in your last letter the direction of our next step. Our next question is: What is the meaning of God's love? What does his love have to do with our adversity and suffering? When we have answered this question, I think we shall have come to the end of our quest. And we shall see, Mark, the practical outcome of this position in regard to your question as to what you do about suffering beyond accepting it.

Yours,
Jim

❧ ❧ ❧

March 1

Dear Jim:

I found your four propositions exciting! But they marched along so clearly that I thought on the first reading they were too clear, too easy. I said to myself, "Something must be the matter with this; this is a trick

95

—no religious argument can be as clear as this." But I went over it several times and the impression grew on me that, though we cannot know God entirely, we can, as you said, "see the fringe of his garment." And I said, "This is true—really true!"

A great deal that the Church has been saying is now beginning to make sense. I even think I may one day be able to identify myself with the writer of the hymn, "O Love That Wilt Not Let Me Go," and feel something more than wistfulness and a sense of the hymn's poetic beauty. Then I may be able to see the Cross of Christ as something more than the tragic symbol of death with which the world rewards those who oppose its entrenched evil. Then, too, I may be able, on the level of actual living in my own life, to meet adversity and suffering as something more than necessity which must be accepted. As I write this, I hardly recognize myself.

In regard to the question which you said we should consider next—"What is the meaning of God's love? What does his love have to do with our adversity and suffering?"—I suggest that we put off that question until you have given me your thought on another.

Soon after our correspondence started, I began reading the Bible, feeling that this was the least I could do toward making some contribution. I read it for clues to possible answers to the questions which buzzed in my mind. But now, Jim, without your help handy, I'd give up trying to read it, or confine my reading to those passages which I most readily understand—the sections which speak to man's common, native experience with life and with God, which, as I've heard our minister say, like God himself, is the same "yesterday, today and forever." The Psalms, for example, the Proverbs, Job, the Sermon on the Mount, Jesus' parables, Romans 12, I Corinthians 13.

However, I don't want to give it up. I want to read and understand more of the Bible than its devotional sections and its "wisdom" literature—Proverbs, for example. But I've become increasingly confused and frustrated. You see, I've harbored the notion that I should be able to understand the Bible. Like other laymen, I've gotten that notion of competence from the Church—in insisting that we read the Bible, the Church has led us to assume that it's easy reading. And it's not; it's difficult. Outside the great, well-known passages, I'm lost. But I'm intrigued by the persistent feeling that the Bible is indeed a sacred book, that God speaks in it. Last night I finished the Book of Jeremiah—and found that outside of a few verses and scattered sections, I simply had no notion of what it might mean. And yet I've gathered from the Church that all one needs to understand the Bible is a devout and pious mind. It seems to me, Jim, that the Church has failed to do a job of teaching which affords more than a snapshot view of fragments of the Bible.

I have another and deeper problem which raises a deep doubt. The Church has presented the Bible to the

layman as a unit with an internal continuity. And ye
the Bible is not one book, but sixty-six books, written—
as I've learned from an encyclopedia—over a period o
some twelve hundred years, by many people, for variou
purposes, in several languages, against differing socia
backgrounds. The only thing which holds the Bible to
gether for me—besides the fact that it is, as a whole
about God—is that these books are bound togethe
as one book which I have learned to reverence as on
book.

Thumbing through the Bible the other night, I mad
a few notes on what it contains. It presents without an
inner continuity, a miscellany of stories, ancient re
ligious laws, accounts of tribal and national struggle
lives of patriarchs, heroes and prophets, songs of lov
laments of sorrow, proverbs, sermons, pictures of savag
hatreds, bloody battles and cruelties, enslavements an
deliverances; the armies of Egypt, Israel, Judah, Assyri
Babylon, Persia, and Rome march across its pages. The
time stops; Jesus appears and is seen briefly in Galile
and Judea with his disciples, while around him, seekin
to destroy him, are the Sadducees, priests, Levite
scribes and Pharisees—lay figures for envy, craft an
hypocrisy in the contest of established evil against th
revelation of God.

But it doesn't hang together, Jim. It has no unity i
which the books have coherence and increasing mea
ing.

Now, as part of this problem, there is the clear fact that within the Bible there is actual disagreement. For example—and this is directly related to our problem of suffering—the New Testament says: "God is love." But what does the Old Testament say about God? As pictured in some of the Old Testament stories, God is certainly not a God of love, but a God of vengeance and cruelty, one who shares the tribal prejudices and hatreds of that ancient time. As illustration of this, you will recall the story of the slaying of the Amalekites, "both man and woman, infant and suckling," in I Samuel 15. We now call such genocide a crime against humanity! And why? Because we have had God revealed to us as a God of love; because we have had Christ's injunction laid upon us: "Love your enemies, bless them that curse you, do good to them that hate you, and pray for them which despitefully use you, and persecute you; that ye may be the children of your Father which is in heaven: for he maketh his sun to rise on the evil and on the good, and sendeth rain on the just and on the unjust."

How do you get Jesus and Samuel agreeably together in this holy book? I can accept Samuel's consuming hatred of the Amalekites within its primitive setting, but if I accept Jesus I can hardly accept this ancient story as representing the God who is the same "yesterday, today and forever." And yet—there it is in the Bible. Because of this problem, the Bible falls apart as I read it. So, added to the sheer difficulty of the text in many passages, there is the question of the Bible's authority—for it seems to me that its authority is, to some degree, contingent on its unity.

Let me sum up this question, if I may, Jim. Here is a book held sacred by the Church and elevated as our supreme authority on religious ideas. We are enjoined to read it, and yet no small part of the layman's confusion of religious ideas is due to the fact that the Bible has no clear unity which organizes the layman's thinking.

What have you to say to this problem?

Sincerely,
Mark

P.S. By the way, fishing through the ice was good this winter. Wish you could have been here.

𝕯   𝕯   𝕯

March 10

Dear Mark:

Your reference to fishing so unfitted me for getting down to work that this letter is a day late. Perhaps we may be able to get to some bass fishing this summer.

I quite agree with you that some sections of the Church have failed to be of much assistance to laymen in the matter of reading and understanding the Bible; I agree with you also that the Church has promoted the notion that all one needs to understand the Bible is an attitude of reverence. This admission does not mean, however, that I think one's attitude in reading is of little consequence. The Bible is definitely a closed book to the thoroughly secular mind. But I don't think that's your difficulty.

Your first difficulty, Mark, is that you know so very little about the Bible. To read a book like Jeremiah with understanding, you first of all must know something about the purpose of the book and the setting in which it was a series of living events before it became a book. Then you must have help with the text itself. I am amazed at the otherwise intelligent people who say they cannot understand the Bible and yet will do nothing to correct their ignorance of it. It seems to me that anyone interested in the Bible who is willing to spend twenty-five dollars for a bedside radio to hear some funny man, should certainly be willing to spend a like amount for books which will make the Bible more intelligible! I would suggest that you purchase a good one-volume commentary on the Bible and a copy of the Moffatt translation. With these to help you, go back and read Jeremiah again.

I agree with you further, Mark, that right here is the place to discuss your problem, the unity of the Bible, and your illustration of that problem, the wide difference between Samuel and Jesus. In posing this problem, you have seen how our last proposition, concerning the love of God, cuts directly across some of the stories and conceptions of God in the Old Testament: since God is the

God of infinite love and is the same yesterday, today and forever, he cannot be the cause of suffering and the instigator of the massacre of the Amalekites. (It is one thing to say that we suffer when we run counter to the constituted laws governing life; it is quite another to fly in the face of Jesus' teaching and to say that the extermination of the Amalekites followed God's express command.)

Before attempting to show how the Bible may be brought into some reasonable unity such as you feel and I agree, you need to find in it, I want to give an example of my own of the sharp contrast between the teaching of Jesus—and behind it, Jesus' conception of God—and an Old Testament story. As a growing boy, I had no more trouble with the slaying of the Amalekites—they were the bad men—than I had with my own bloody, though imaginary, slaughter of cattle thieves and bandits in my back yard. But sometime in my teens, I came across the following story in II Kings 2:23, 24: "And he [Elisha] went up from thence unto Bethel: and as he was going up by the way, there came forth little children out of the city, and mocked him, and said unto him, Go up, thou bald head; go up, thou bald head. And he turned back, and looked on them, and cursed them in the name of the Lord. And there came forth two she bears out of the wood, and tare forty and two children of them." And this story was in the same book, the Bible, which told how Jesus gathered the children about him and blessed them!

That story of Elisha's curse jarred me wide awake to this problem. How are we going to bring Elisha and Jesus agreeably together? Is our God the God who Elisha believed would back his curse? Of course he is not. Our God is the Eternal, the God and Father of Our Lord Jesus Christ, the same yesterday, today and forever—not understood by Elisha, but known and understood by Jesus. Let's tack that down.

But perhaps you are asking about the two she bears which came out of the wood, and tare forty and two children? I would say that that is the clincher—it fixes our rebellion against the story, particularly against the implication that God sent the bears to back the angry prophet's curse. Even admitting the historicity of this attack on the children, we may be very sure that the coming of the bears was a coincidence. And what a terrific coincidence! But I have heard it argued that God did indeed send the bears to punish the children and that if one does not believe that he should not say that he accepts the Bible. I know of no one who really takes all of the Bible as an authoritative guide in personal living. We certainly do not accept as authoritative for ourselves the ethics of the whole Bible—the polygamy of the patriarchs, Jacob's deception of his brother and his father, the Old Testament treatment of defeated enemies, the eye for an eye treatment of those who offend us. And we certainly do not allow the Old Testament to limit our beliefs—in immortality, for example. (In this connection, see for yourself the contrast between

103

Psalm 88:4-12, Ecclesiastes 3:19, 20 and 9:4, 5 on the on
hand, and I Corinthians 15:35-44, 53-55, on the other.
These differences between the Old and New Testamen
cannot be dismissed; and if the Bible is to have any unit
it must be a unity which reckons with and encompasse
these differences.

Jesus himself made clear his departure from some o
the beliefs and practices of the Old Testament, and i
we attempt to level off these differences, we shall fail i
availing ourselves of the revelation of God in Christ. So
in dealing with this problem of suffering, let us kee
clear our belief that God, as revealed in Christ, is love
We must allow no picture of him in the Old Testamen
to obscure that!

What, then, shall we do with the Old Testament
Shall we abandon it altogether, because we find in i
conceptions of God which do not agree with the rev
elation of God in Christ and ways of thinking and
living which we, as Christians, cannot accept? Of cours
not. Jesus did not abandon the Old Testament; he used
it, especially the great, prophetic insights; he tran
scended the limitations of the Old Testament. Following
him, we need not hesitate to place the Old Testament i
proper perspective behind him in history and to see th
Bible for what it is—the record of the long journey o
man with life and with God, wherein the revelation o
God comes gradually and at last fully in Jesus Christ.

You are correct in saying that the Bible must hav
some sort of coherence and unity for the reader. T

satisfy this need, he may be quite prepared to accept the theory of unity which is most simple and is ready at hand. This is the the theory which imposes on the Bible the sort of unity which it does not have—a unity of equal revelation and authority, which runs from first to last, from Genesis to Revelation. I have thought that this theory is best represented by a straight line, thus:

X———————————————————————X

This theory holds the Bible together for the devout reader by flattening out its internal differences of idea and concept and making its authority as absolute, revealed truth equal throughout—and this in spite of the fact that Jesus himself refused to accept the limitations of the Old Testament. I suggest in this connection that you read Matthew 5, noting especially the sections beginning, "Ye have heard that it was said"—his reference to parts of the Old Testament and to the traditional interpretations.

Now, to be sure, all Christians say they accept Jesus Christ as their final authority in the interpretation of Scripture; but this acceptance has not always operated for them to place the Old Testament into proper perspective. It appears to me that once the authority of Jesus Christ is truly accepted and his teaching and spirit, with the doctrine of his person, become a fixed point of reference from which the Old Testament is judged, the unity of the Bible is seen to be not in the sameness of its teaching, but in the continuity of the

revelation of God which runs upward through the dif
ferences and disagreements and comes at last to com
pletion in Jesus Christ. Such unity may be represented
thus:

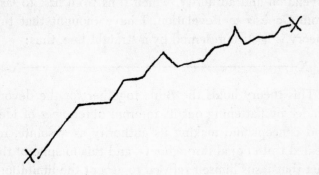

This diagram, I hope, suggests the idea I want to pass
on to you. The ascents and plateaus—and the retro-
gression—have here no reference to specific Bible passages; the point of the diagram is that the unity of the
Bible lies in the ascending, progressive revelation which
may be traced in it in respect to the great ideas and
conceptions of God, man, sin, redemption, righteousness,
worship, immortality and suffering. The revelation was
not constant or continuous—there were temporary ret-
rogressions, lapses, when understanding and acceptance
lessened rather than grew. The diagram illustrates this
fact.

The Bible as a whole, when viewed from our vantage
point, is a series of documents written in the changing

context of history and containing ideas, ethical standards, and social patterns which scholars can now stratify
in relation to historical periods and to one another. As
another has suggested, the unity of the Bible as a record
of God's revelation is like that of the coming of light—
first the murky dawn which penetrates the early mist,
struggles through recurrent darkness, and at last comes
to unclouded splendor in God's revelation of himself in
Christ. In this deep and real sense the Bible is the Word
of God.

This approach to the Bible is of great importance in
dealing with the problem of suffering. We have said
that "God's relation to us in our world is determined by
his nature and purpose." Now, with our understanding
of his nature as revealed in Christ no longer obscured
by the limited conceptions of God found in the Old
Testament, we understand that his love is boundless and
constant. The God in whom we believe is the God and
Father of our Lord and Saviour Jesus Christ; in dealing
with this problem of suffering, we hold fast to that and
allow no lesser conception of God's nature and purpose
to influence our thinking. "For God, who commanded
the light to shine out of darkness, hath shined in
our hearts, to give the light of the knowledge of the
glory of God in the face of Jesus Christ" (II Cor. 4:6).

Well, Mark, there is my answer to your question about
how we can bring the Old and New Testaments together
into some understandable unity. I know it is not a full

answer—you will have to get a more complete picture
of the unfolding revelation from the Bible itself and
from reading beyond this meager letter. I have tried to
give here a principle of approach. If it does not satisfy
you for the time relative to our major purpose, or raises
further problems, tell me.

Yours,

Jim

⑨ *⑨* *⑨*

March 18

Dear Jim:

Your way of approaching the Bible and getting the
Old and New Testaments together is of great help to
me. My first and last comment was, "This makes sense."
For the first time in my life, the Bible as a whole is coming
to have meaning. As to my ignorance of the Bible—I'm
certainly going to try to correct that. In fact, I've already made an outlay of cash, as you suggested, to back
that resolve! I've bought a copy of the Moffatt translation and a one-volume commentary on the Bible, which
I see will give me the background of Bible history,
special articles on the religion of Israel, and so forth, and
interpretive comments on the text of the Bible itself.
Elisha and his curse of the children won't trouble me
now. This stopover has been very worth while.

Now, let's get back on the main track. In the last
paragraph of your letter of February 26, you wrote: "Our

next question is: What is the meaning of God's love? What does his love have to do with our adversity and suffering?"

It seems to me, Jim, that the first part of your question is useless. I don't see that God's love needs an explanation or description to give it meaning. It's like the love of parents for their children—and everyone knows the nature of it, so why labor at trying to describe it? You don't describe it—you simply accept it. Isn't that so?

However, I think that something needs to be said here about what God's love has to do with our adversity and suffering, for I still feel that it is remote, a sort of behind-the-sky sentiment on a grand scale. I'll never be able really to sing about it until I have some inkling as to what it does. I guess that's what I want to know at this point: what does the love of God do?

I must get on to the greenhouse now. Thanks, again, for working this out with me.

In haste,
Mark

🕭 🕭 🕭

March 26
Dear Mark:

I feel that you are really taking hold of this matter now—especially since you have spent some money on books to back your resolution to correct your ignorance of the Bible!

Quoting from your letter, you say that the love of God "is like the love of parents for their children—and everyone knows the nature of it, so why labor at trying to describe it? You don't describe it—you simply accept it."

That seems to be a sensible remark, but it isn't true to experience. The fact is that many of us have never really grasped the meaning of being loved by our parents. We have taken it for granted—as we have the fact of having been born. And just as the love of parents is taken for granted, assumed and not really understood by their children for what it is, we are very apt to feel that the love of God is, in your words, "a sort of behind-the-sky sentiment on a grand scale," a general sort of love we attribute to God because he is God, just as we attribute love to parents because they are parents. We accept it in much the same way, but do not inquire into it, appreciate it for what it is, nor really respond to it. We allow the statement that God loves us to remain a theological assertion.

But fortunately, the time comes for us children—perhaps not until we have grown old—when the love of our parents for us is appreciated. Then, in humility and gratitude, we really love them. And when is that fortunate time? When at last we see that, because of their love for us, our parents are deeply involved in our lives—that no pain or loss of ours is ours alone, but is theirs also, that no growth, no gain, no learned skill or hard-won attainment, no happiness of ours is ours alone, but is theirs also, shared by them. Sometimes this insight dawns on us in later years when we remember how proud they were of our little attainments when we were children; then, in burning memory we recall how embarrassed we sometimes were by their attention; we understand then that we did not appreciate their love, for we were not yet equipped by experience to understand what it means to be loved.

Let us now ask our question again. What is the nature of God's love? Ask our Lord and he replies simply that God is our Father; he tells us the story of the son who went into the far country and wasted his substance in riotous living, whose father saw him returning while yet a great way off, ran to meet him, embraced him, brought him home, clothed him and celebrated his return. The father's life is bound with that of his son into one bundle; he is deeply involved in it, has been hurt through it and is at last delivered from that hurt only when his son is delivered from his suffering and waywardness and is at home again. Jesus says to us that God is like that father; his love is a father's love.

In dealing with this problem of suffering, Mark, we must take seriously this teaching of Jesus as to the nature of God's love, for if we heed his teaching as the revelation of God, another face entirely is placed upon our problem, the problem of suffering. According to this revelation, God's love is not an abstract love, remote and objective to our hurts—such love, even by human standards, would be no love at all. It must be a love which, by its very nature, involves him as our Creator in our life so that he shares with us its hazards, its suffering, its defeats, its growth, its attainment and its joys.

Admitting the limitation of analogy in trying to state the meaning of God's love, I still find this analogy entirely convincing in the central truth it makes clear: *we and God are companions in risk and sharers together of the suffering entailed in the creation of persons.* In stating this, we have come a very long way from our starting point; we have arrived at an answer. Our next step it to make clear the meaning of this answer in terms of experience. But I must leave that for another time.

You said in your letter of March 1 that you hope to see the Cross of Christ "as something more than the tragic symbol of death with which the world rewards those who oppose its entrenched evil." Do you begin to see its meaning now?

Sincerely,
Jim

☞ ☞ ☞

April 2

Dear Jim:

I must get down to Washington soon!

I hardly know what sort of reply to make to your last letter, except to say that I found it curiously exciting. I say "curiously," because I cannot imagine the Mark Fisher you knew before the war—and the Mark Fisher I lived with and thought I knew—finding excitement in this sort of thing. Beside the world of facts and events with which I was then preoccupied, this would have seemed just so much fanciful stuff. (Or would it? On second thought, looking back to that time, it seems to me that I would have come to the place where I am now if our correspondence had taken place then, for it seems that I have always been asking the questions which projected me into this inquiry.)

You ask if I am beginning now to see the meaning of the Cross. I think so. The Cross is a symbol of God's involvement in man's life, not only its sin, but also its hazard, adversity and suffering. As symbol, it serves to hold before us this truth; without the symbol of the Cross, the truth of God's involvement and active participation would easily fade from the mind and be lost beneath the endless details of life. The Cross stands for me as a single, comprehensive statement of God's love.

Is this good Christian theology?

Sincerely,
Mark

✿ ✿ ✿

April 7

Dear Mark:

Congratulations! You are now really on your way and running under your own steam; and I sense in your letter not only the excitement of your new insight into Christian theology, but the fact that you are becoming, as you said some time ago, my co-protagonist.

I quite agree with you that the Cross, as a symbol, serves the purpose you indicate. But in my view, the Cross is more than a symbol, Mark. The Cross is a divine, creative event in history. I believe that in the suffering and death of Christ, as well as in his life, God took into himself and upon himself the burden of human life, with its hazard, its sin, adversity and suffering. In Paul's phrase, "God was in Christ, reconciling the world unto himself."

What then, is "acceptance of Christ"? It is the acceptance of God's love in Christ, by which our transgression is covered and its eternal consequences annulled. But it is not only acceptance of Christ's death as atonement, but acceptance of his life as the Word of God made flesh, which, as such, becomes our highest authority. Such acceptance is like the homecoming of the Prodigal Son and deals with both the past and the future: it redeems us from the worst consequences of our freedom as persons and restores us as sons of God and creators together with him. Thus, we are saved—in every way—not by ourselves, but by God; and knowing this, we will walk softly because of the wonder of redemption, but we will walk with security and with expectant anticipation.

This packs a deal of theology into two paragraphs. I suggest, Mark, that you now read the New Testament, beginning with Paul's letter to the Romans.

Yours,

Jim

Dear Jim:

I have not yet digested your two packed paragraphs of theology. But I've started the reading you suggested; and we surely will discuss this matter again—perhaps on some fishing trip. Look at your schedule and suggest a date. Sometime in July? I know a mountain lake. . . .

Going about my work, I'm preoccupied with this idea: The notion that the Almighty, the Eternal, the Creator of the stars, so shares life with us as to suffer its risks and defeats seems only a hairbreadth from being an absurd fancy. But yet, I see that it must be so! Else our first surmise and growing persuasion of his reality is dead wrong, and back of this world and the universe there is nothing but blind chance. That I cannot believe! And this hairbreadth is enough for me, for the idea is not absurd once we see that his creation of persons must be, by its very nature, a real, creative venture and a risky one in which God is involved.

The process of creation, any creation, is always, at some point, a risk, isn't it? Even a blacksmith, in the simple process of making a horseshoe is confronted by the dead resistance of his materials—and, if he will go on, he is risking a burn from the fire. How far beyond the making of horseshoes is the creation of persons—and what a vast difference in the risk involved! It is like creating a child, who becomes a person in his own right, with intelligence and desire. The child may, if he chooses, oppose his father's will and break his father's heart; he is free to do so. Our blindness to this lies in our failure to see in the word creation anything more than a word and our failure to believe that God really did create man in his own image, with freedom—dangerous freedom—in his own right.

Now, I think we must come to grips with the question of what we do with all this. We have said that the purpose of God's enterprise is to create persons, that such creation entails risk, adversity and suffering which he shares with us because of the very nature of his love, his involvement in our lot. What is the practical outcome of this view in one's personal religion, that is, in one's way of life?

Sincerely,

Mark

𝕀   𝕀   𝕀

April 21

Dear Mark:

Your question indicates the direction of our next step. In answering it, I want to say first that this insight into the problem of suffering cannot be experienced without at the same time setting up a new attitude toward life. I mean that a new attitude follows the insight. The realization that God is in this with us throws on the problem of suffering—and on suffering itself—a new

116

light, even puts another face on it; and this changes our attitude toward life's hazards and toward all of life including those parts of it which are shadowed by risk, and even toward that final valley of the shadow. We become, in the words of Paul, "ready for anything."

Now, this change of attitude is not simply due to an experience of companionship with God, though that of itself is a wonderful experience; added to this knowledge that we are not alone, there comes to us a new knowledge of the significance of adversity and suffering in terms of what may come out of them: we see what is at stake and are able to grasp the fact that the hour of adversity may well be either the hour of creation or the hour of destruction in respect to God's purpose and our destiny.

Let me illustrate this. Illustration here faces the possibility of failure in two ways—if the illustration is unusual in our experience, it is not convincing, and if it is commonplace, its point is apt to be too obvious to have significance. I'll take the latter risk.

The common cold is for me a particularly insidious form of misery and spiritual risk because of what it can do to me behind my back while my attention is centered on its symptoms. Its results are not simply nasal discomfort and congestion—I get over these. But beyond these, see the power of the common cold! It can make me impatient, crotchety, cross-grained, sink me in a bog of self-pity, make me insensitive to the needs and even the rights of others and irresponsible to the tasks and commitments to which I should hold myself. I say things I should not say, adopt attitudes which confuse my friends and in my home relations make mountains out of molehills and upset my children—all of which I tend to excuse in myself, but cannot quite excuse in others. The fact is that I may never recover from these results of the common cold: they become part of the person who is me, expressing themselves again and again when I face other sorts of adversity. Thus, you see, when I have a cold, I must somehow get my attention off its symptoms and realize what is really at stake.

This is a simple illustration of the fact that the principal issue in any sort of adversity is what it may do to character and personality, that is, to the person. Come at it either from theology or from the practical considerations of psychology and we come to the same conclusion: the most important thing to do about adversity and suffering is not simply to bear it—though that is difficult enough—but to consider intelligently and prayerfully what it may lead us over a period of time to become. That is the issue. God, whose purpose is the creation of persons, is concerned with that; and that should be our chief concern. Only as that is our chief concern will our attitude toward life be such that we shall be able to handle adversity with a positive intention in respect to how it is to affect us and those around us.

You will be saying now that it is very difficult to see this as our chief concern, the chief issue, when we are caught between the sharp jaws of adversity. Indeed it is! How easy it is then to be preoccupied with pain, or loss, or other elements of our trouble, to take a negative attitude toward it, to feel that God has turned his back on us, ceased to love us, or even sends us the adversity which bedevils us, forgetting that he never ceases to love us, not even when we flout what we are quite sure is his will. How easy it is then to pity ourselves, to think that the universe, or fate, or the stars are against us! How long will it take us to eradicate such notions from our thinking and feeling and to realize that God's love for the lost and wandering and hurt is constant and un-changing?

The view I have advanced not only changes our atti-tude toward life, it makes clear what the will of God must be. This is of great practical value in living the Christian life in respect to handling trouble. People who are ill are sometimes admonished by sincerely pious folk to submit to God's will. But what is God's will for such folk? I am sure it is not that they suffer. God himself is their companion in suffering and as he bears it, they must bear it, too. His will is, rather, that in suffering they shall be creators with him and that out of it there shall come some new, shining facet of personal quality. That is his will and purpose—and their highest destiny.

The truth of this is realized, of course, by many who

never have stated this position systematically as we have done. It is realized intuitively and by the inspiration of the Holy Spirit by many great souls whose lot it is to suffer most. For example, I know a woman who has suffered the tortures of arthritis for twenty years and is every day an inspiration to her friends and an exemplar of this truth. She has every reason to become a sour, cantankerous old woman; but no word of rebellion or self-pity is heard from her. Though her body has been twisted out of shape by the disease, she has grown in beauty and stature of spirit. Many visit her, not to comfort her, but to be comforted in their own lesser troubles. She tells them that she has a secret: she is not alone and not idle. Of course she is not idle—she and God are together engaged in a creative task, an event of eternal significance: *the creation of a person and all that may mean in the context of society—and eternity.*

"But," you ask, "is it never God's will that we shall suffer for a good cause?" Indeed it is—when the alternative is retreat, the saving of oneself and the sacrifice of others, or the compromise or defeat of that good cause. We are then indeed called to suffer; suffering is then dedicated suffering, willingly accepted. In this connection, I recall the strong comfort and challenge given by Matthew Arnold to those who complain of the forces arrayed against them:

> They out-talked thee, hissed thee, tore thee?
> Better men fared thus before thee;

Fired their ringing shot and passed,
Hotly charged—and sank at last.

Charge once more, then, and be dumb!
Let the victors, when they come,
When the forts of folly fall,
Find thy body by the wall!

Jesus chose suffering when he refused to leave Jerusalem and seek safety; he chose to die if need be, rather than to live. This resolve is shown in his prayer: "Oh, my Father, if this cup may not pass from me, except I drink it, Thy will be done." But let us not believe for a moment that God killed Jesus, or that God caused the martyrdom of his saints. Sin, treacherous, envious, fearful sin killed them.

You are asking, perhaps, if God is never against us? Certainly, he must often be opposed to what we choose and what we do, but he is never against us. He loves us with an eternal love; and so far is he from being against us, that he is counting on us! FOR, WHEREVER THE HUMAN SPIRIT MEETS ADVERSITY, THERE MAY BE THE GROWING POINT OF GOD'S CREATION. In that hour, we and God face together not only hazard, but spiritual opportunity; there the issue is the creation of the best and the most in human personality.

So, you see, the main issue of life is not whether we die, or live on in comfort, not what becomes of us, but what we become. Though it would be foolish to say that growth in greatness of spirit and character cannot be forwarded when life smiles on us, it is still true that situations of adversity place such growth in special jeopardy and that through them and how we handle them we make slow or sudden passage from what we are to what we shall be. Thus, creation waits on that moment. That's a sobering thought, isn't it, Mark?

Sincerely,

Jim

ɷ   ɷ   ɷ

April 30

Dear Jim:

I now see what you meant some time ago when you wrote that I'd be wise to stay away from my customers when I'm feeling crotchety and impatient, but that there is "a more excellent way of dealing with the spiritual hazards of the common cold." There is, indeed, a more excellent way. In this connection, I want to suggest that there are spiritual hazards peculiar also to comfort and success. For me, the hazard of success is that I shall think more highly of myself than I ought to think, with the result that my view of my relationships is distorted and my judgment is warped. I have noted, too, that at such times my ego declares holiday and lets into my soul a whole troop of little devils—which, without him to sponsor them, might not gain admission.

Relative to your last letter, I have several questions at this point, Jim, which will have to wait till we may sit down together for a lengthy discussion. But there is one which will hardly wait. You say that God "loves us with an eternal love; and so far is he from being against us, that he is counting on us! FOR, WHEREVER THE HUMAN SPIRIT MEETS ADVERSITY, THERE MAY BE THE GROWING POINT OF GOD'S CREATION." Then later on you say that through situations of adversity and how we handle them "we make slow or sudden passage from what we are to what we shall be." But what of the man whose life is cut off, robbed of this chance of making passage to any future whatsoever? Suppose he is killed by this adversity, what then?

Sincerely,
Mark

🕮 🕮 🕮

May 5

Dear Mark:

I wish you had put a sharper point on your question. As it is, it applies to everyone, for we are all "killed," in one way or another by adversity, that is, by circumstances which might be counted as adversity. At whatever time in life we die, we are "cut off." But are we? You see, your question is really one about immortality.

I presume that you were thinking of the death of a

young person—a soldier, for example, who dies in battle almost before he has had a chance to live; and not having further chance of life and growth, and no opportunity to become the sort of person he might have become, his destiny and God's purpose are apparently unfulfilled. The death of the young, for this very reason, seems particularly sad.

I suggest, first, that fulfillment of one's destiny—to become, as persons, the best and most that is possible for us to be, to the glory of God—is not entirely contingent on length of life. Methuselah's biography, despite his long life, is a very brief one: "And all the days of Methuselah were nine hundred sixty and nine years: and he died."

I suggest further that we have no way of knowing what actually has been accomplished, created, in the space of a life. We judge a man by the outward signs of character, though we have no way of knowing absolutely the person he has become relative to what he has been; we know nothing of his soul, of the aspirations and flashing dreams, of the tensions and struggles, and growth. But we judge him just the same; we put a label on him, tagging him with failures which are obvious by our own standards. But God mercifully "looketh on the heart"—for that we should be thankful.

I have suggested, Mark, that your question is really one about immortality. I do not propose to argue about this; but I have two thoughts which may be useful to you.

First, as another has suggested, our greatest difficulty in believing in immortality is not with the intellectual problems it presents, but with the failure of our imagination—we cannot picture immortality. In all our experience we have known no life which has not been embodied in some visible form and we therefore cannot imagine life without a body such as we have known. In this connection, I suggest that we have never seen life itself—it always has been invisible; we have seen bodies, but not life. So, life takes its place in that category of invisible realities which are the very "stuff" behind this visible creation. Certainly in our day, it should not be difficult for us to believe in the reality of the unseen—we talk glibly of unseen electrons, protons and neutrons, we utilize unseen realities every time we tune in our radios. To be sure, the reality of these unseen "patterns of electrical energy" is no argument for continuance of life after the death of the body, but the admission that unseen reality exists should save us from slamming shut the door of our minds against its possibility.

My belief in immortality, however, rests on a much more firm reason. I believe in God. I believe in God's existence, greatness, purposefulness and love. I believe that he has capped his creation by the creation of man and that his love involves him with us in the whole event of life. And though I cannot picture immortality, I find it impossible to believe that this purposeful, loving God can be dealing here in simply temporary and transient matters. (You see, Mark, how this goes back to our early argument in which we refused to believe that there is nothing but blind chance behind the universe?)

So, in answer to your question "what of the man whose life is cut off, robbed of this chance of making passage to any future whatsoever?" I say, in summary, that we do not know, as God knows, what has happened to him, what he has already become and created in the course of his life—perhaps he has already made passage to that future which we think has been denied him. And further, he has not been "cut off," discarded; his life is in God's hands.

Yours,
Jim

    ☙ ☙ ☙

May 11

Dear Jim:

This correspondence is doing something to me—I am looking at life differently, rather, I think I am just beginning to see it. For example, when I first wrote to you and raised the problem of God's relation to suffering and adversity, I was thinking in terms of bodily suffering, illness, injury, death and material loss. But just these hazards and the way we handle them do not comprise the whole event of becoming and what we become. There are other hazards, often so subtle as never to enter our awareness as important factors in the making up of our lives and our selves: longing and denial, frustration of purposes, "death of dreams," feelings of inadequacy, conflicts with people, conflicts within ourselves, the stubborn opposition of the materials with which we work, the long difficulty of acquiring skills, monotony and the feeling of staleness, slights to our egos, temptations, the loss of youth, advancing age and the feeling of uselessness. These are all spiritual hazards, are they not? And we are made by the way we see them and deal with them. Their strength lies in the fact that we so often fail to see them for what they are!

Now to get back again to the main theme. We have said that God counts on us in adversity so to handle trouble that—like the woman with arthritis—we grow in spiritual stature. This is my question at this point: When we, in turn, count on God, when we trust in him, what can he do?

It seems to me this is a very important question. Let me expand it a bit. Is not the help God may give us limited by the very conditions which he has established as necessary for the creation and growth of persons? May we expect him, in order to help us, to break through, or set aside, the regular working of natural law, the necessity of human learning, the freedom of human beings to choose, and the togetherness and interdependence of persons? Is he not committed to the irrevocable working of these factors which are not only the causes of suffering, but the very factors without which the creation and growth of persons is impossible? If God is so committed, what can he do besides suffer with us? And, if he is so limited, where is this partnership in creation we have talked about?

I think this puts the question as clearly as I can manage it.

Sincerely,
Mark

ı *ı* *ı*

May 16

Dear Mark:

I'll reply to your question within a day or so. At the moment I have time only to add a comment to your observation on the multiplicity of life's spiritual hazards.

As you say, we often fail to recognize and appreciate our spiritual hazards for what they are; and worse, failing to appreciate them, we make occasional great preparations for a spiritual stand in battle on some Maginot Line where we propose to "defend our ideals" and "resist the devil," only to be outflanked and defeated in the small behind-the-line encounters which we are not prepared even to see. We hear great sermons on discipleship and in hymns and formal prayers gird ourselves for the great moments when battles shall come. Then, busy with "practical" matters, we fail to realize that already we have lost a dozen decisive skirmishes behind the

lines of our formal resolves. So it is every tragic day
when we fail to realize where the spiritual battle lies—
we think that the struggle with the devil is a phony war!

Hastily,

Jim

❦ ❦ ❦

May 19

Dear Mark:

I am asking for your patience; you have asked a theological question which calls for a rather lengthy theological answer, but I hope that, by this time in our adventure, you will find it not a tedious one.

You asked in your last letter: "May we expect him
[God], in order to help us, to break through . . ." and so
forth. When you use this expression, "break through,"
you are begging the question as to whether God needs
to break through, or set aside, natural law in order to be
active here. Your question arises, you see, in the assumption that, in relation to the universe, God is an outsider.
It isn't necessary to assume that, you know.

At the risk of oversimplification, I suggest that there
are three ways of conceiving of God's relation to the
universe and to us. These are known in the history of
theology as deism, pantheism and theism.

Deism assumes God, as you have assumed him to be,
as outside our lives and the conditions in which we live,

as absolutely transcendent, dwelling in a sort of fourth-dimensional eternity, having no active relation with the reality in which we dwell.

Pantheism identifies God with the universe—he is the universe and in no way objective to it.

Theism is the conception that God is real and objective to the universe which he has created; God is not simply the sum of man's best ideas and impulses, but is best to be thought of as a person, who has revealed himself to man and has real relationships with man in history and in the experience of individuals. (I find it impossible to think of God except as a person. Some may be impatient with me here, saying that God cannot be limited by this anthropomorphic conception. My reply is that, if we are not content to think of God as something we call ɪᴛ, we must think of him in the highest and most meaningful term permitted to us by human language. And how can we escape the limitations of our language? It seems to me that our best course in this matter will be, not to try to escape it, but to use it. So, I think of God as a person; and, as a Christian theist, I believe that God has revealed himself in the Bible and primarily in the living event which lies behind it; I believe that he has revealed himself supremely in Jesus Christ, the Word of God made flesh.)

Now, when we place the deist's conception of God in relation to the other conceptions—particularly in contrast to theism—we see that it (deism) is really a conception of God's absence rather than of his presence and that it sets before us the dilemma which you stated.

But we need not make the assumption which poses this dilemma. Instead of thinking of God as totally outside our universe—and consequently as having to "break through" if he is to have real dealings with it and us, let us think of God as inside. I do not mean, of course, that we should think of God's greatness as held and confined in the universe which we know. God dwells in eternity; but my point is that he dwells also in time. God is so really within the universe—in it as we are in it—that we need not think of him as having to "break through" and to shatter its basic structural framework and order to be active in it in our behalf.

You see the value of this conception relative to the question you have raised? However we may think of God as transcending his creation, it seems to me that there is essentially no more reason for thinking of him only as beyond and outside it than there is for thinking that we, self-conscious beings, are outside it. Let me explain this a bit further. The principal value of the idea of God's transcendence is that it expresses in language our certainty that God is, in every conceivable way, limitlessly great; it expresses our conviction of his greatness by helping us to hold in language the realization that he cannot be bound to our space-time, or other limitations, or by any limitations, except those set by himself, by his own nature.

But transcendence need not mean that God is outside the universe, as deism conceives him to be—and as certain theologians of our time seem to think him; nor does it mean that he must "break through" to be active here. Consider this, Mark: we ourselves transcend the material universe in some degree—we are self-conscious beings who are not only in the universe, but because we view it objectively and understand it as not ourselves, we do transcend it.

You may object here, Mark, saying that we do not transcend time and space. In a sense we do! We have memory of the past and imaginative vision and anticipation of the future—thus, we transcend time-present. And through imagination, memory and understanding we transcend even the spacial limitations of physical vision at this moment. When we realize this, we begin to take seriously for the first time the Biblical revelation that God created man in his own image. And since transcendence such as we have is thus a God-given endowment of human personality, the notion of deism—that transcendence places God beyond and outside the universe—is untenable. It doesn't place us outside the universe. And furthermore, that notion is certainly not Biblical; in the Bible God is simply present.

Now, let's gather this up. As deism errs in one direction, pantheism errs in just the opposite. Pantheism conceives that God is in everything and identified with everything from stars to corpuscles and atoms—God is the cold which freezes, the heat which consumes; he is energy, electricity and light. So, where deism loses God by remoteness, pantheism sentimentally loses him by diffusion. I don't believe he need be lost to us at all! He is simply here and theistic personal religion rests upon this assurance. So, as Tennyson puts it—in a poem curiously enough titled, "The Higher Pantheism":

> Speak to Him, thou, for He hears, and
>   Spirit with Spirit can meet—
> Closer is He than breathing, and nearer
>   than hands and feet.

Now to meet the point of your question as to how God acts in our behalf. It appears to me that he acts with us —and against us!—and beyond our ken, through the four factors which together constitute the structural base of life and the framework of human personality— through the operation of natural law, through the intricate and unpredictable possibilities of individual and racial learning, through our choices and the making of our choices, and through the indescribably complex relations of human beings.

You may ask in this connection what happens to the conception that God acts "supernaturally." I fail to see that this conception is at all jeopardized, for I am saying simply that God uses for his purposes the forces and elements of the universe which he has established. By definition, God's activity must always be supernatural; and to insist that God must break and violate the fabric of his creation in order to be active here is to make a very large assumption which limits God in one's belief. It is exactly for this reason that many otherwise devout people in our day say that "the age of miracles has passed."

According with my whole position, I say that God is active here. The age of miracles is still present with us and I will not presume to set a limit in my belief as to what God may do. Therefore, I look for him on every hand; I look for tomorrow with great expectation! Faith in God is this very expectation and the prayer of faith is not simply a breath upon our lips, a weak voice lost in the clatter and roar of the real events of the world; it is itself an event and the means of creative alliance with him.

Yours,

Jim

❡ *❡* *❡*

May 25

Dear Jim:

I have a nostalgic memory of myself as a small boy kneeling by my bed and praying:

> Now I lay me down to sleep,
> I pray Thee, Lord, my soul to keep;
> If I should die before I wake,
> I pray Thee, Lord, my soul to take.

I still have—and feel—other prayer memories: small-boy petitions, prayers for things, dutiful requests that God bless the members of my family, "thank you" prayers, pitiful little confessions. Though I can't recall the words of these prayers, the memory of them is a shaft of light in a dim room.

Then somewhere along the way of growing up, I quit praying and left it to the minister.

But though I've left praying to the minister for many years, I admit that several times when life has been too much for me, I have attempted, quite uncomfortably, to pray. I suppose that this is a quite common experience, even for people who attend church regularly—in fact, it seems to me that attendance at church and having one's prayers said by a "professional" makes it easy for the layman to abandon personal prayer, even though he still theoretically believes in it.

Why do laymen like myself leave praying to the minister? I don't quite know, except that it is difficult to cross the gulf between theory and practice. Part of that difficulty is that our beliefs are so fuzzy, lacking relevance to the experience and reality which are the stuff of life. Added to this is the fact that praying seems to have a language and a style of its own; that is, part of the difficulty is in the proper saying of prayers. As most of us attempt it, praying is a verbal performance.

Now, your statement that prayer is an "event" intrigues me. I take it you mean that prayer is not just something in our heads, but is an objective event, as real as walking somewhere, or throwing a ball, or firing a gun. Surely, you don't mean that the wandering of a sleepy mind at bedtime, the thoughtless repetition of a learned prayer, the halting words that I might address to the Almighty have the power to make a difference in the world? I can't believe it. Though my beliefs are not hazy and confused as they were and though I have many real concerns which I believe are God's concerns, if praying has to be the saying of prayers, I'm afraid, Jim, that I just can't do it. I'd bog down in a sense of unreality.

And yet, I've lately found that the written prayers of others can become my own. Some days ago I purchased two little books, *A Diary of Private Prayer* by John Baillie and *The Temple* by W. E. Orchard. I found myself reading these prayers with the sense that they were mine. That's odd, isn't it? I can't pray, but I can use the prayers which have been real to others—I say real because I'm sure that the prayers in these books were, as you suggested, living events and that, when I appropriate them, they are so for me. I don't understand that at all. Of course, these prayers are beautifully composed. But are they just words? Or are they something else? Am I becoming a mystic? I can't believe that!

If you wish, Jim, leave this matter of prayer for discussion over a campfire. I have a suggestion. Could you get away July first for that fishing trip? I think I mentioned a mountain lake I've fished several times; but let's go back to the Kawarthas. Do you remember?

However, when you write again, you might give me a summary of the long way we have come.

Sincerely,

Mark

ﻬ　ﻬ　ﻬ

June 2

Dear Mark:

The Kawarthas it is! July first.

I think it would be more profitable for you to make the summary for yourself. But, for what it may be worth to you until you get around to doing it, here is a brief reminder of the high points.

We began with the statement of the problem of adversity and suffering: how are we to reconcile our belief in an almighty and all-loving God with the suffering of God's children? And what is there to say concerning God's relation to the destruction or jeopardizing of the very values which, it would seem, should be the object of his love and protection?

Finding the common, pat answers unacceptable, we concluded that God is not the cause of human suffering and then accepted Fosdick's observation that the immediate causes of suffering and adversity are four: 1) the operation of natural law; 2) the progressive nature of human life—that is, that life is embraced in a learning process which in itself may be hazardous and without which human beings suffer or could not survive; 3) the operation of man's freedom to choose; 4) the togetherness of human life, the interrelation and interdependence of persons, because of which suffering and adversity will not stay at home, but travel through the social relationships of life.

You rightly said that we had not solved our problem, had not made the universe just a "dandy place," by generalizing the immediate causes of suffering—whatever the immediate causes, we are still stuck with our dilemma. Why did God establish these four causes in the first place and thus assign to man his "outrageous fortune"?

I indicated that, in asking this question, you were proposing that God should have made another sort of universe, and I suggested that we consider what a universe and world closer to heart's desire might be. We finally concluded that these four factors are not only the cause of man's suffering, but the source of all his blessings and constitute together the only conceivable setting in which the human spirit and character may emerge and grow. Thus, as you accepted the four causes, you "accepted the universe." In this connection, I wrote: "It is important to note here, Mark, that this acceptance of the universe is not merely academic: on the level of living where our attitudes arise, the universe is indeed ours for rejection or acceptance. If we reject it, we go increasingly toward confusion and frustrated rebellion; if we accept it, we are on our way to further insight as to its meaning, we form an alliance with it and from this alliance there may arise a new life for us. (This is essentially what happens for many people through simple faith in God.)"

At this point, you went back to your original question, but put a sharper point on it: What is God's relation to this process of the creation of persons? How is he related to our suffering and to us?

My answer was that God's relation to us is determined by his nature, and I then put forward four propositions: 1) if, following our surmise that there is a God behind the universe (rather than simply blind chance), we say that God exists, then we must say that he is an unimaginably great God—greatness is a corollary of his existence; 2) granting his greatness, he must be a purposeful God—purposefulness is a corollary of his greatness; 3) since God established the four factors which together constitute the setting of man's emergence and growth, his purpose must be the creation of persons; 4) since God is a God of purpose and his purpose is the creation of persons, he must be a God of love—his love is a corollary of his purpose. (I suggest, Mark, that you turn back in our correspondence to get the full force of this argument.)

There followed a discussion of how God's love is best

described and we said, as Jesus implied in speaking of God as our Father, that God's love, by its very nature, involves him with us in the risk and hazard, the adversity and suffering, as well as the growth and glory of human life. To sum this up: ". . . a God great enough to have created this universe, a purposeful God who has crowned his creation by the creation of persons in his own image, must be a God of infinite love, else he were monstrous. It is impossible to think of our God as not caring for his creation. Love is a corollary of his greatness and is on the scale of the universe itself, limitless, beyond our power to grasp, concerned beyond our power to appreciate. This, of course, is what the New Testament teaches: 'GOD IS LOVE.' "

God's purpose—the creation of persons—is our destiny and though growth of the best and most in human life may take place in any circumstance, in fair weather as in foul, suffering and adversity are clearly a battlefield on which the issues of life come to point and the destiny of the human spirit are at stake. Wherever the human spirit meets adversity, there may be the growing point of God's creation, for the hazard of adversity presents itself also as spiritual opportunity. There we and God are companions in adversity and the risk it entails; there our chief concern should be, not what becomes of us, but what we become through this experience by which we make passage from what we are to what we shall be. Thus, our destiny and God's purpose wait on how we handle adversity, how we live with pain, on what disappointment makes of us. And, in adversity, we should not think that he is against us, for so far is he from being against us, that he is counting on us! We are creators together with God of the shining facets of the human spirit with which it is his purpose to cap his creation: thus, it is our destiny "to glorify God and enjoy him forever."

At this point, Mark, you asked your important question as to whether we may rightly expect God, in order to help us, to "break through," or set aside the four factors in his universe without which the creation of persons is impossible.

My reply was that God does not have to break through, that he is not the outsider you have assumed him to be: "However we may think of God as transcending his creation, it seems to me that there is essentially no more reason for thinking of him only as beyond and outside it than there is for thinking that we, self-conscious beings, are outside it." Since the measure of transcendence we have does not place us outside the universe, the notion that God's transcendence places him outside the universe is untenable. God is present; and we are not alone.

I then said: "It appears to me that he [God] acts with us—and against us!—and beyond our ken, through the four factors which constitute the structural base of life and the framework of human personality . . . I look for him on every hand; I look to tomorrow with great expectation! Faith in God is this very expectation and the prayer of faith is not simply a breath upon our lips, a weak voice lost in the clatter and roar of the real events of the world; it is itself an event and the means of creative alliance with him."

This brings me to your last letter. You have raised questions here which would commit us to correspondence for months to come. But fortunately, we shall soon have opportunity for lengthy discussions, as you suggest, over our campfire. However, to tide us over till that happy time, I should like to make several brief observations on your experience with prayer.

It seems to me, Mark, that you have put your finger on your difficulty and that of many other people. You have been thinking of prayer as primarily talking, as a verbal performance; and at the same time you distrust words as a means of communicating with the Almighty. Certainly, prayer as a verbal performance may not always commend itself to an honest mind; it may have nothing back of it, express nothing and really deceive no one. Such prayer can hardly be the sort of real event which is the means of a creative alliance with God.

I think we must begin by taking seriously our God-given endowment of freedom as persons. We have the prerogative of living our lives by ourselves, without God; and we may be sure that God, who created us as free persons in our own right, will not abrogate that freedom. If he is effectually to have a part in our lives, we must open our lives to him; prayer is the means by which we do this and become partners with him in the creation of the persons we may become according to his purpose and our destiny. Moreover, prayer is indispensable if we are to use the hazards and adversities of life as occasions, not only for our own spiritual growth, but also for the furtherance of God's purpose through us in the society with which we are so closely interdependent.

You are fortunate to have discovered the two little volumes of prayers you mentioned in your letter. (They very effectively give the lie to the slander that religion is necessarily a retreat from life!) But, because you have found that these prayers can become living events for you when you appropriate them, you are puzzled, for you have learned to distrust verbal prayers. Are these prayers not just words, you ask, like other words? Or are they something more than words? My reply is that they were once something a great deal more than words and that they may be so again whenever anyone like you can make them his own. Now, what is that something more?

I suggest that real prayer begins, not in speaking, but in "seeing," in a spreading out of life before oneself and God. Until this is done, we really have nothing to speak about, we have no reason for words. The "something more" that makes the prayers of Baillie and Orchard real events when you appropriate them is that they do this for you in your private devotions. They reveal your past, still alive, but dim and half remembered, your present, of which you may be unaware, and your future as you doubt it, fear it, or hope it may be. Through these prayers you see your life and consequently in using them you have a sense of reality.

You say that, if prayer is just the saying of words, you cannot pray. I am saying that if you are to pray you should not try to begin with words, but with the seeing of life in God's presence.

At this point, Mark, I feel this should be illustrated, but that a hypothetical illustration would prove of little value; therefore, I am taking the liberty of using an illustration which may well be from your own life.

As a father, you probably know by this time that a father and son may live in the same house and share the same blessings, but may rarely meet; they may have—depending on the size of the house—a close proximity, but no real community of life. They are two individuals who may each go his own way; and for convenience and comfort's sake, and because of his pressing preoccupations, the father is quite apt to let the son go it alone.

Suppose you are this father. One day an event in your son's life brings him startlingly to your attention. In a moment, because you love him, you are acutely conscious of your involvement in his life. There are several things you may do; you may "talk to him" as a father and you may make certain wise arrangements to meet his problem; you may even boost his allowance! But helping him is difficult, for you can't get quite near enough to him; he has been growing without your notice and it is later than you think. What, then, can you do to help him and yourself? I suggest that you pray for him—that in faith you spread out life, his own and yours, before you and God: you see that your son is trying to grow up inside, as well as out, that he has crossed the rim of a new, strange world; you know, from your vantage point in maturity and from your own green memory, that he has problems which he cannot now understand; you look at these problems and at him and you know the truth which can make him free; he wants to break through the conventions, but he doesn't, he is frustrated and uncertain in his choices; you see his relationships with people and what they have the power to do to him; you see that you have often dealt with him without understanding, you have withheld your own insights and resources; you see the person your son is now and the kind of person that he may, with God's help and your own, grow into; you see his times of strength and certainty being enlarged, growing as he grows; you see him coming to endure the hard day of adversity; you see the growth of character he needs to forego the passing pleasure and to live for the lasting value. . . .

And the important thing, Mark, is that you know you are not alone in doing this; you are in partnership with God in a creative enterprise. This praying for another is known as intercessory prayer. It is not just the common-sense understanding of another's life; it is an event which, by faith, has the power to change life. It not only does something to you in terms of your understanding, it does something to and for your son. Though as objectively real as walking to some determined place, it is a mystery too deep for description. And note, Mark, that, engaging in it, you may not have spoken a word. (But why should you not now use language, since you have so much reason to use it?)

Similarly, the other recognized elements of prayer may all be experienced—thanksgiving, confession, supplication and aspiration. Such prayer is much more than tugging at one's psychological bootstraps; it is more than trying to be happy in spite of one's sins; it is more than wishful thinking; it is more than words.

Real prayer which begins with seeing may be a rigorous experience. In it we experience tension of a peculiar sort; we raise the tensions of life into attention and take a firm, deliberate grasp upon them. We see them for what they are: conflicts within ourselves between the actual and the ideal. For the most part, Mark, we live our lives between these two worlds: the actual job and the ideal one, the actual salary and the one we want, the house we live in and the one we dream about, the health we have and the health we long for, the persons we are and the persons we wish in our best moments to become, the people we live with and the people we think they should be. These, the actual and the ideal, are millstones which can crush us and grind us to powder.

Let us admit that we are not big enough or resourceful enough to stand between them alone. Only God, who is the God both of things as they are and of things as they may become, is great enough for that place. And he is with us there: we are not alone. Together we become partners in this event of prayer and in the creative enterprise which we are free to share with him—and have him share with us.

So, we end our present journey, Mark. But it is not journey's end: I'll see you when we go to the Kawarthas, where the pines grow straight at the edge of quiet water.

Yours,

Jim

P.S. Soon after we began our correspondence, you said you were surprised I did not refer you to a reading list. I'm a bit surprised myself. As I recall, you have already purchased a one-volume commentary on the Bible and a copy of the Moffatt Translation of the Bible. (Don't neglect the introduction in the Moffatt translation.)

Reading in theology and adjacent fields of study is likely to be slow business; but I think it will be more immediately rewarding for you now than it would have been a year ago.

Below is a list of books which are rather closely related to the ideas we have been discussing. I'm not listing them as supports for my thesis in our correspondence, but as a means of further acquainting you with the fields of thought we have touched. I don't agree with all you will find in them—and I'm sure all the authors do not agree with me. Therefore, I'm not suggesting that you attempt to swallow them whole and absorb them. Use them as tools for your own thinking and living, and to push back your horizons.

BAILLIE, JOHN. *Diary of Private Prayer.* New York: Charles Scribner's Sons, 1949.

BENNETT, JOHN C. *Christian Realism.* New York: Charles Scribner's Sons, 1941.

BOSLEY, HAROLD A. *A Firm Faith for Today.* New York: Harper & Brothers, 1950.

BOYER, MERLE W. *Highways of Philosophy.* Philadelphia: The Muhlenberg Press, 1949.

BUTTRICK, GEORGE A. *Parables of Jesus.* New York: Harper & Brothers, 1928.

CARNELL, EDWARD J. *The Theology of Reinhold Niebuhr.* Grand Rapids, Michigan: Wm. B. Eerdman's Publishing Co., 1951.

DUNOÜY, LECOMTE. *Human Destiny.* New York: Longmans, Green and Co., 1947.

FOSDICK, HARRY EMERSON. *A Guide to Understanding the Bible.* New York: Harper & Brothers, 1938.

―――. *On Being a Real Person.* New York: Harper & Brothers, 1943.

―――. *The Three Meanings: Prayer, Faith and Service.* New York: Association Press, 1950.

―――. *As I See Religion.* New York: Grosset and Dunlap, Inc., 1947.

HEDLEY, GEORGE. *The Superstitions of the Irreligious.* New York: The Macmillan Co., 1951.

HORTON, WALTER M. *Our Christian Faith*. Boston: The Pilgrim Press, 1947.

JAMES, WILLIAM. *Varieties of Religious Experience*. New York: Longmans, Green and Co., 1938.

JONES, RUFUS. *The Luminous Trail*. New York: The Macmillan Company, 1947.

————. *New Eyes for Invisibles*. New York: The Macmillan Company, 1943.

————. *Spiritual Energies in Daily Life*. New York: The Macmillan Company, 1949.

JUNG, C. G. *Modern Man in Search of a Soul*. New York: Harcourt, Brace and Co., 1933.

MACKAY, JOHN A. *A Preface to Christian Theology*. New York: The Macmillan Company, 1941.

MILLER, RANDOLPH C. *Religion Makes Sense*. New York: Chicago: Wilcox and Follett, Co., 1950.

MOFFATT, JAMES. *The Bible: A New Translation*. New York: Harper & Brothers, 1935.

MORRIS, DANIEL L. *Possibilities Unlimited*. New York: Harper & Brothers, 1952.

NICHOLS, JAMES H. *Primer for Protestants*. New York: Association Press, 1947.

NIEBUHR, REINHOLD. *The Nature and Destiny of Man*. New York: Charles Scribner's Sons, 1943.

ORCHARD, W. E. *The Temple: Book of Prayers*. New York: E. P. Dutton and Co., Inc., 1946.

STEWART, GEORGE. *The Church*. Hazen Books on Religion. New York: Association Press, 1940.

WHALE, J. S. *Christian Doctrine*. New York: Cambridge University Press, 1941.

WALKER, WILLISTON. *A History of the Christian Church*. New York: Charles Scribner's Sons, 1918.

The Abingdon Bible Commentary. Nashville: Abingdon-Cokesbury Press, 1929.

The Interpreter's Bible, Twelve Volumes. Nashville: Abingdon-Cokesbury Press, 1951.

PHILLIPS, J. B. *Letters to Young Churches, a translation of New Testament Epistles.* ed. New York: The Macmillan Company, 1948.

Set in Linotype Caledonia
Format by T. E. Mergendahl, Jr.
Manufactured by The Haddon Craftsmen, Inc.
Published by HARPER & BROTHERS, *New York*